WINNING WITH FINANCIAL DAMAGES EXPERTS

A Guide for Litigators

RONALD G. ROSENFARB

CLAYTON GILES

Published through Ingram Publisher Services LLC

ISBN: 978-1-68419-308-0

This book is dedicated to my mother, Sharon, may she rest in peace; my grandfather, Henry, who will always be one of my heroes; and my grandfather, Frank, who is a real mensch and an amazing man – *Ron Rosenfarb*

To my late parents, Leonard & Elizabeth Giles, and Si Yoon and Emma, my wonderful wife and daughter – *Clay Giles*

CONTENTS

INTRODUCTION

Thank you for opening the cover of this book. We hope you find the information educational and valuable. This is a book for lawyers, especially commercial litigators. The information in this book will surely benefit your practice. Our intention is to provide guidance and knowledge regarding how to gain the most value from using financial experts. We've learned from the best professionals that we know when is best to retain a financial expert, how financial experts can provide value for your clients, and we've obtained valuable insights for interviewing financial experts.

This book consists of interviews of 15 well-respected, highly experienced, and very bright professionals conducted over the course of a year. Thirteen of these professionals are attorneys and two are experienced forensic accountants whom have testified as experts in numerous cases. Each chapter is a transcript of an interview.

In these interviews, many of the responses we received were similar. They stated that while litigators should hire experts very early in litigation, even before pleadings are filed, most, if not all, typically do not. They are concerned about their clients incurring fees. Many of the attorneys used the word "facile" when describing what they look for in how a testifying expert responds to direct and cross examination. "Quick on their feet" is a phrase that was also used quite frequently. All of the attorneys interviewed wanted an experienced financial expert with previously qualified expert testimony. Few cared how many times the expert testified for the plaintiff's side as opposed to the defendant's side.

One frequent comment was that attorneys want to retain an expert they really like – someone they could be friends with. Of course, this makes perfect sense.

If the attorney does not like the expert, how can he expect a judge or jury to like him? The attorney will also be spending a significant amount of time with the expert so it's necessary for them to get along with one another. This is not a baseball game where a team signs a pitcher strictly because he throws strikes and has a great change-up. In litigation, you want the best expert, but you must also pick and choose an expert tactically, strategically, wisely, and be practical in whom you select. The expert must be a good "fit".

We believe by the end of reading this book you will have gleaned more knowledge regarding the use of financial experts than you had when you picked it up. The bottom line is that when you use the best financial expert who fits in with your team, more often than not your client will be awarded more money or owe less money.

Thank you again for reading our book.

Wishing you many successes,

Ron Rosenfarb

Clay Giles

ABOUT THE AUTHORS

Ronald G. Rosenfarb was raised with a forensic accountant as a father. His dinner discussions growing up centered around his father's cases and what he and his brothers thought about those cases. Later in life, after becoming an attorney licensed to practice in New York and New Jersey, Ron joined his father's firm, Rosenfarb LLC. He spent nearly a decade working there as a lawyer and forensic accountant. In 2017, he left Rosenfarb LLC to embark upon a new journey as an entrepreneur. Ron resides in San Juan, Puerto Rico.

Clayton Giles is an attorney and forensic accountant at Rosenfarb LLC. In 2013, he joined Rosenfarb LLC, a firm of forensic accounting and valuation experts with offices in New York City and New Jersey. He has over 15 years of litigation experience. Prior to joining Rosenfarb, Clay was lead counsel in numerous state and federal court actions involving complex commercial litigation matters while at Fox and Fox LLP. He also worked at Milberg LLP, a class action and securities litigation firm. Prior to law school, Clay was an accountant for Trebron Management, formerly GynCor, Inc., a physician practices management company headquartered in Chicago. Clay is a former Judicial Law Clerk for the Honorable Roger M. Kahn of the Tax Court of New Jersey. He resides with his wife and daughter in Brooklyn.

ABOUT THE INTERVIEWEES

Jorge A. Amador is an attorney, certified public accountant, certified in financial forensics, and certified fraud examiner. He has over 20 years of corporate and public accounting experience. In 2011, Jorge became a Director at Rosenfarb LLC, a firm of forensic accounting and valuation experts with offices in New York City and New Jersey. He has testified as a financial damages expert in many matters. From 2003 through 2007, Jorge was the Director of Forensic Accounting at Milberg LLP, a class action and securities litigation firm. Earlier in his career, he worked in public accounting where he planned and directed audits of manufacturers, financial services companies, and construction contractors. Jorge taught a graduate course on forensic accounting at Baruch College, and he was co-chair of Practising Law Institute's Accounting for Lawyers 2-day conference. Jorge resides in San Francisco.

Lawrence Carnevale is General Counsel at Teneo, a global CEO advisory firm that works exclusively with CEOs and senior executives of some of the world's leading companies. Prior to joining Teneo, Lawrence was a partner and head of the litigation pactice for Carter Ledyard & Milburn LLP, where he also served as a member of the firm's Executive Committee. At Carter Ledyard, his practice focused on general commercial litigation. Lawrence has authored many articles and spoken on a variety of legal issues, particularly concerning the financial services industry. Lawrence is a graduate of Dickinson College, cum laude, and Temple University Beasley School of Law, cum laude.

Harvey S. Feuerstein is a partner and chairman emeritus of Herrick, Feinstein LLP. He served as chairman of the firm's Executive Committee from 2001 to 2012 and previously as chair of the firm's Litigation Department. He has more than 50 years of litigation and arbitral experience. Harvey concentrates his practice on business divorce, representing owners who seek to profitably disengage from their associations with successful businesses and firms. Harvey received his A.B. from Columbia College at Columbia University and his J.D. from Harvard Law School.

John Goldman is a Director of the Venezia Football Club, an Italian football club from Venice, Italy, and founder of JRG Business Solutions Corp., a business consultancy firm. Venezia F.C. is a professional Italian soccer team that plays in Serie B, the second-highest division in the Italian soccer league system. Prior to launching JRG Business Solutions Corp. and becoming a Director of Venezia FC, John was a senior partner in Herrick, Feinstein LLP's litigation department and co-chair of its Sports Law Group. John received his B.A. in Economics from University of Michigan and his J.D. from Benjamin N. Cardozo School of Law, Yeshiva University.

Peter J. Gutowski is a partner of Freehill Hogan & Mahar LLP. He has more than 30 years of litigation and arbitral experience. Peter focuses his practice on international and domestic transportation matters. He has served as lead counsel in many high profile transportation related casualty and contract disputes around the globe. He also serves as a commercial arbitrator, has presented papers and made presentations on corporate veil piercing, security proceedings, and fraud claims, and he co-authored the U.S. section of the Shipping International Trade Law text published by Sweet & Maxwell, a division of Thomson Reuters. Peter received his B.A. from Columbia University and his J.D. from Tulane University Law School, cum laude.

Martin E. Karlinsky is the founder and managing partner of Karlinsky LLC, which he launched in 2012. His practice focuses on commercial and civil litigation. Marty is a seasoned trial lawyer with over 160 jury and bench trials, arbitrations, and appeals. He has almost 40 years of experience. In 1982, Marty founded Camhy Karlinsky & Stein LLP with William L. Scheffler, and served as managing partner of the firm until 2000 when he became a partner and senior counsel of Rosenman & Colin LLP and its successor firm Katten Muchin Rosenman LLP. In 2009, he joined Butzel Long, P.C. where he served as managing partner. Harvey teaches trial advocacy with the National Institute for Trial Advocacy. He received his B.A. from New York University and his J.D. from University of San Francisco School of Law.

Gerald Krovatin has more than 30 years of experience of trying criminal and civil cases. In 2007, he formed Krovatin Klingeman LLC with former federal prosecutor Henry Klingeman. He is a graduate of Columbia College and Rutgers School of Law, Newark. In 2003, Gerald was admitted as a Fellow to the prestigious American College of Trial Lawyers and the International Academy of Trial Attorneys. He is also the former President of the Association of the Federal Bar of New Jersey, and he taught the Criminal Trial Seminar at Rutgers Law School as an Adjunct Professor of Law for four years. Gerald is the author of Caution Flags For Corporate Managers, 12 Cardozo Law Review 1291 (1991).

Bryan H. Mintz is a partner of Mintz & Geftic, LLC. He focuses his practice on complex litigation, involving contract and business disputes, products liability, class actions, medical malpractice, and personal injury litigation. Prior to joining Mintz & Geftic, Bryan was a partner of Paris Ackerman & Schmierer, LLP. Prior to Paris Ackerman & Schmierer, he was a senior litigation attorney at McCarter & English LLP. Bryan earned his B.A. from Rutgers College and his J.D. from Rutgers University School of Law. After law school, he worked as a judicial law clerk for the Honorable Robert Muir, Jr., Presiding Judge of the New Jersey Appellate Division. Bryan has been selected to the New Jersey Super Lawyers list every year since 2014.

Sam Rosenfarb, CPA, ABV, CFE, CVA, CBA is the Managing Director of Rosenfarb LLC, a firm of forensic accounting and valuation experts with offices in New York City and New Jersey. Sam has more than 40 years of business and accounting experience. In 1990, he created the forensic accounting firm Rosenfarb & Co. which merged to form RosenfarbWinters, LLC in 1999. In 2008, RosenfarbWinters merged with a top 20 CPA firm where Sam was Partner-in-Charge of the forensic accounting practice. Sam established Rosenfarb LLC in 2011. Sam is frequently retained by clients to provide deposition and trial testimony. Throughout his career, he has testified as an expert witness in numerous matters, including damage calculations, matrimonial litigation, accounting malpractice, estate matters, partnership disputes, business valuations, and insolvencies. He has served as a court-appointed expert and arbitrator, including appointment to the Panel of Arbitrators by the American Arbitration Association. Sam is a recognized industry expert and has presented seminars and continuing legal education courses on various topics, including calculating lost profits, valuation techniques, mergers and acquisitions, valuation aspects of divorce, forensic accounting, and alternative dispute resolution. He hosted the cable television programs "White Collar Crime Report" and "It's All About Money." Sam resides in New York City with his wife Marilyn.

Paul H. Schafhauser is a partner of Chiesa Shahinian & Giantomasi PC. His practice focuses on complex commercial and contractual disputes involving real estate, insurance, intellectual property, and business dissolutions. Prior to joining Chiesa Shahinian & Giantomasi, Paul was a partner of Herrick Feinstein LLP and counsel to a large real estate development company in the New York metropolitan area. Earlier in his career, he worked on Wall Street at Merrill Lynch and Salomon Brothers. Paul is a contributor to New Jersey Foreclosure Law and Practice, a seminal treatise on foreclosure law. He received his B.S. in Finance from University of Pennsylvania and his J.D. from Boston University School of Law.

William F. Sondericker is a partner of Carter Ledyard & Milburn LLP. His practice focuses on representing Japanese controlled enterprises engaged in business in the United States and providing personal representation of business entities, shareholders, and individuals in business transactions, arbitrations, and trials. He also serves as an arbitrator and federal court mediator. William received a B.S. from New York University and an LL.B. from The Catholic University of America (Law Review).

Seth T. Taube is a partner of Baker Botts L.L.P. His practice focuses on securities and commercial litigation, SEC and state attorney general defense, corporate governance, and white collar criminal defense. Seth has over 40 years of trial experience, and he has served as Branch Chief of Enforcement at the New York Regional Office of the SEC. In 1982, he was awarded the Manuel Cohen Distinguished Lawyer Award by the Commissioners. He also served as a Special Assistant United States Attorney in the Securities Crime Unit of the United States Attorney's Office for the Southern District of New York. Seth teaches International Trade Law at Benjamin Cardozo School of Law, and he has taught courses on mergers, acquisitions, and corporate litigation at Seton Hall Law School.

Jantra Van Roy is a partner of Zeichner Ellman & Krause LLP. She is co-chair of the firm's bankruptcy and business insolvency practice and leads its structured finance litigation practice. Jantra has almost 30 years of experience in asset recovery litigation, bankruptcy, and out-of-court loan restructuring. She has served as lead counsel for major European and American banks in complex multi-party actions. She has also worked closely with Thailand's Ministry of Justice to draft the country's comprehensive new business reorganization laws. Jantra was selected as one of only two attorneys to serve on the American Bankruptcy Institute panel with U.S. Bankruptcy Judges to deliver private lectures to the Thai Supreme Court.

William D. Wallach is a partner of McCarter & English, LLP. His practice focuses on commercial litigation, including representing companies and their management in connection with their fiduciary duties and statutory obligations, and member and shareholder disputes in closely-held entities. He has been appointed as a Monitor, Receiver, and Special Fiscal Agent by Chancery Judges in New Jersey, and he has spoken on various topics, including Article 2 Sales Issues for Lawyers and Non-Lawyers, Disputes Involving Closely-Held Businesses, and Expert Testimony Issues for CPAs.

Jeremy Wallison is a partner of Wallison & Wallison LLP. His practice focuses on trial court, appellate, and arbitral litigation of complex business disputes. Jeremy writes and lectures on emerging issues in business law. He received his A.B., cum laude, from Harvard University, where he was awarded the Harvard College Scholarship, and his J.D. from the New York University School of Law, where he was a Leslie and Edmund Glass Fellow.

CHAPTER 1

JORGE AMADOR

Ron: I'm with Jorge Amador. I am writing a book on how to win - how litigators win their matters using financial experts. Jorge is not only an attorney, but he's been a forensic accountant for many years.

Tell me just a little bit of your background - how many years you've been an accountant, how many years you've been an attorney? The reason I'm interviewing you is to get the experts' point of view and how you've worked with litigators.

Jorge: I was a traditional accountant. I worked for mid-sized to large regional firms in public accounting, primarily on the audit side. I also had responsibility for overall client review, like looking at their tax compliance; we'd do business consulting and do the audits. So I was responsible for overall client services.

I did that from 1985 to around 2000. But in the late 90s, I started doing forensic accounting primarily in connections with construction litigation. But there was never any testifying or anything like that. It was just basically auditing claims that the contractors would submit to the owners.

Sometime in the late '90s, I became involved in a case between two doctors. Somebody from my office said, "you're going out there, the attorney has questions, start reviewing the documents." I started doing that and a few weeks after I was helping him and he said to me, "oh, you know by the way, you're going to be testifying in a few weeks."

Ron: And that was a shock too?

Jorge: I wasn't expecting that. It went from having a very nervous experience to really enjoying the process.

Ron: What made you enjoy the process?

Jorge: The difference between doing an audit or doing a tax return is that people review it and they may have questions on it. But nobody ever really challenges you on the tax return. If you put together an expert report, there is somebody on the other side that's looking to, basically, take your head off.

It was the closest thing to competitive sport that there is without being physical. It's an intellectual battle. You've said these particular things and the other side is trying to discredit you and trying to say you don't know what you're talking about. It's competitive; it's a fight.

Ron: I'm going to ask you a few questions that are normally presented to the litigator; I'm going to ask you the same type of questions and have you answer as a forensic accountant.

Jorge: I also worked at Milberg Weiss part of the time as a litigator.

Ron: Milberg Weiss was a large plaintiffs' firm in New York City and they had other offices, right?

Jorge: Right. Offices in LA, San Francisco, Boca Raton, Tampa, Florida, Seattle.

Ron: And they settled cases for billions of dollars while you were there, correct?

Jorge: Right.

Ron: So, one of the largest areas of what the financial experts do is opine on financial damages. I know forensic accountants can be economists that are professors or something in academia. And some forensic accountants are currently in the practice of public accounting, and some are professional expert witnesses. The sort of disputes that are appropriate for the retention of a financial expert, in general, are business disputes, IP disputes, accounting malpractice claims, and other disputes over money and valuations.

        How would litigators find you as an expert to interview you and decide if they want to retain you?

Jorge: There are a few ways. One is client relationships that I've had before. They'll reach out to me and say, "oh, we have this case. It's similar to another case you've worked on. We'd like you to work on it." That is the direct relationship.

        Then there are referrals from partners or associates that I've worked with before. They say that, "Jorge worked on that particular matter and he was really helpful; you should use him for your next case." Those are the two main sources for me.

Ron: I imagine that's going to be consistent throughout how litigators find their experts, they either worked with them or they've been referred by somebody they trust.

Jorge: Right. Because litigators are looking to get very precise on the sort of experts that they use, they're using expert referral services.

Ron: When you say precise, you mean niche forensic accountants?

Jorge: Right. It could be they're looking for somebody in the oil and gas industry or somebody in the retail industry or somebody in an industry of focus.

Ron: We had this discussion today interestingly, how forensic accountants get put in a box. You're put in that box. You know oil and gas, you're the oil and gas guy. So you can't possibly be the real estate guy.

Jorge: Right.

Ron: But that's disheartening to me because if you're a forensic accountant and you're determining lost profits; I would think that unless it's something maybe like art and antiques, which is a different type of niche, that you could opine on lost profits in any industry.

                How do you feel about that? I see that there is a general direction towards hiring somebody who's in a specific niche.

Jorge: What I've noticed with the cases that I've worked on here, or when I was at Milberg; if you're working on a telecom case, there are certain things obviously that are precise to telecom industry or whatever it happens to be. But it's not so much about money or the financial aspects of the case. It's more about the technical, as in telecoms: the optics, the wire, and all that stuff and obviously you can't opine. Forensic accountants can't opine on that sort of thing.

                But when it has to do with money, the forensic accountant can opine about that. Just like an auditor will have clients in the service industry, retail, construction, manufacturing; you learn about the industry. A lot of times, when a litigator hires somebody who's a so-called expert in a particular niche; they lack a certain freshness than somebody who deals with a lot of different practices brings to the table.

                For example, when I worked on a Maritime case, we looked at cases that went back to the 1700s. We brought a certain freshness and intensity to learning about all the things that were relevant to the case. For example, we learned what an allision was. When it came to financial aspects, all the relevant issues that were necessary to be able to opine on the finances, on the damages issue, we found and there was a sort of a freshness. I wasn't there at the testimony for the other expert. But I would imagine that he had a certain overconfidence about what he knew about the particular industry because he was always in it.

When we get a case from when somebody who works on different matters, I think that, if they're good like we are; you bring freshness and integrity to every project you take. Because, for me, I enjoy learning about a new thing and want to do a great job.

Using somebody who has a particular specialty can work in some cases. But in other cases, it can hurt you because there is that lack of freshness and there is an arrogance that "I'm so and so" and I don't really need to worry so much about it. If you have somebody who's forced on a day to day or project to project basis, to really learn about the case, the relevant issues, and the relevant industry; it has been successful in the past. Those combinations of things should go a long way.

Ron: When litigators are talking to you, do they want to challenge or ask about your credentials? Is that important to them? Do they want to know you're a CFE?

Jorge: At a minimum, they want to know that you're a CPA.

That's the threshold question.

There wouldn't even be a discussion if there wasn't that credential. CFE is another niche credential; an add on. But I think the CPA is the most important thing with judges and arbitrators because it's a recognized profession with a certain level of standards and knowledge.

I remember being in-house at Milberg and we would be on a call. The lawyers would say, "also on the line is Jorge Amador". The first thing that they would say is he's a CPA in the firm. That was the big thing. They always said that.

Ron: Because that would distinguish you as being an expert in accounting?

Jorge: Exactly.

Ron: As opposed to just the law.

Jorge: Right, exactly.

Ron: Has it hurt you or helped you that you're actually in practice and not in academia; you're not a professor with a PhD?

Jorge: I think in some cases, it hurts. In high profile cases you're looking at particular accounting issues where it's more in the accounting field with issues of liability; not so much damages. I think in damages, it is not so much of a big deal. But on the liability side, where you have somebody who's written books on audit processes, it is a big deal.

Ron: And you're talking strictly about accounting malpractice, right?

Jorge: Right.

            In my point of view, those individuals who have taught and written books and who are professors in that area seem to have an edge. I know that from the litigators that I've worked with when it comes to testifying, those are the people that they're looking for in those sorts of cases.

Ron: Because they seem more sincere to the judge or the jury, or they seem more credible or knowledgeable?

Jorge: They seem more credible in terms of knowledge of the subject area. I have worked on hundreds and hundreds of accounting cases. I was looking at revenue recognition variable interests. You name the sort of case, and I've worked on it in great depth. A lawyer would probably look at me as a consulting expert in a situation where a professor, like Doug Carmicheal, who was at Baruch College and was the Chief Accountant at the Public Company Accounting Oversight Board, would be looked at for somebody to testify on those sorts of matters.

In the damages context, I think it's your ability to testify. And I don't think it's as relevant as the professorial criteria.

Ron: Are you often asked how many times you were testifying or consulting on the plaintiff's side versus the defendants' side?

Jorge: Yes. Generally, in a deposition, the other side will ask.

When they retain me, I don't remember that question so much in the retention.

Ron: But always in the deposition?

Jorge: Always in the deposition. Not only how many times have you testified for the plaintiffs, how many times have you testified for the defendants and how many times have you testified in cases involved with that particular law firm.

That's a fair question.

Ron: You could be the best in the business or you could be their hired gun.

Jorge: Right.

Ron: Have they ever asked you how many times your side won before they retain you? The side you were working on plaintiff or defense.

Jorge: They don't seem to be that aggressive in that sort of question. They'll ask, what cases have you worked on? What cases have you testified in? Or have you been deposed? Have you testified in court and was it an arbitration?

I often volunteer that final thing - testified in arbitration, we won this. And so I'll bring that up.

The other thing that they will ask is if you have ever been disqualified in a Daubert motion.

Ron: What are some essential traits and characteristics that you think you possess or other good forensic accountants possess? What I mean by that is they're analytical, responsive, confident, and detail-oriented. I don't want to put words in your mouth, but those are just some traits and characteristics.

Jorge: Yeah. I think that initially, a lot is about the relationship that you have with the person that you're working with or the person that they've referred you to. Your credentials on paper and what you tell them about the cases you've worked on is what gives them the confidence to retain you. First is the relationship then the confidence to retain you.

I've had people that I haven't met that have retained me that have asked me how old I was because he said I sounded so young over the phone. They may want to know if you have grey hair; I've had that sort of thing.

They prefer somebody who seems to have more maturity. Once you've been retained, I know from being on the litigation side, there are few things: responsiveness and clarity. An expert that's wishy-washy on the issues could be a problem for that litigator going forward. Another issue is clear writing.

Nothing is more frustrating than getting a report that's hundreds of pages long and you can't make any sense of it. I've been involved in cases where the law firm rewrites the expert's report because it's just a nightmare which can lead to other problems going forward. So responsiveness, clarity, objectivity - which is a better word for wishy-washy - and then good writing.

Then all those traits are transferred over to when that individual testifies.

Ron: That leads into my next question. What are the core skills you think should be required of a forensic accountant? Clear thinking and thinking on your feet, I believe, would be good skills.

Jorge:	Exactly. The expert explains to the attorney what does and does not make sense as well as what area he can support the attorney in. I've seen situations where the litigator will force the expert into a particular sort of thing and it doesn't work out.
	You have to have somebody who is able to explain himself and say these are the reasons why if you go down this road, it's not going to work out well. But some experts get put into that situation.
Ron:	Which makes it important to have a clear litigation strategy that you're on the same page.
Jorge:	Exactly.
Ron:	How do you stay calm during cross examination because I see that the litigators can't wait to "get you"? I literally saw a litigator the other day in New Jersey jumping up and down yelling at the expert, "but didn't you say this?"
Jorge:	It's a game; he's trying to get you off your game. He's trying to push you. It's like when you play football and you're on defense, and the quarterback is calling audibles to try to get you offside, or they're doing all these things to trick you.
	You have to be disciplined and focused so that you don't get caught up in the heat of the moment. He's trying to antagonize you, get you off your game.
	You have to remember it's part of the game what they're trying to do. And if you fall into that, you've blown it.
Ron:	Right, they've won.
Jorge:	You've gone offside.
Ron:	Right, that's a good analogy.

Ron: At what point in a case, or maybe they're still deciding whether they're going to take it, are you retained as a financial expert? And when do you think you should be retained?

Jorge: I think that the best time to get brought in is at the pleading stage where you can help them. For example, in an audit malpractice case. I would say that there are very few lawyers who understand what GAAP and GAAS is. Who understand GAAS - Generally Accepted Auditing Standards - the way that somebody who's practiced for 15 years doing audits understands GAAS.

It's not only what you read in books, but it's the actual practice of auditing. What litigators I work with will say, well, what was happening? What were the pressures? What was happening during this time of the audit? What was the auditor thinking about? And those answers you can't get from a book.

There are some litigators who have worked on many auditing cases and know audit malpractices cases well. But those are few and far between. The general commercial litigator is not going to understand the subtleties. So you start out with a great complaint and where you have solid references to auditing and accounting guidance. It raises the credibility of the complaint and shows the defendants that you're on the right target.

I think right at the very beginning is the time it makes sense. And then, you get to the pleading stage and then you have discovery. There are many times where we get brought in after discovery and we find that the information that they received is inadequate where they could've asked for information maybe in native format. We could help them with those sorts of things.

Not only is it more effective in their litigation, but it's also more efficient. It's a lot more efficient to review documents in a native format than to get documents that have been printed and then scanned and then put into PDF's.

Ron: When you say native, you mean so you can get the metadata?

Jorge: Correct. Get the metadata. And then also to be able to see what the defendants were seeing - how were the workpapers laid out.

Ron: Got it. The formula is in the excel spreadsheet.

Jorge: Right.

Also, you can see who signed off on the workpapers. You can see how they were performing the audit. But once you get it in printed then scanned; the people that are doing the scanning are not careful to ensure that it's a complete production so columns may be missing. It creates a whole bunch of potential issues.

The native format allows the forensic accountant to perform analysis from those documents without having to re-input information. A lot of times there's lots of information that was produced as PDF, but could've been produced in the format that allows the forensic accountant to analyze it in a much more efficient way.

What happens is that usually the accountant is retained once they've received those documents. And that is probably too late.

Ron: The best time would be to bring him in the beginning of the pleading stage. But in reality, they're probably not brought in until much later, correct?

Jorge: Right, because there's this expectation that the case is going to settle. "Oh, we're going to file a complaint, we're going to have a meeting, they'll give us a few documents and the case will settle." Two or three years later, they have documents sitting in their office. They say, "oh, we're going to send them over and nobody's really looked at them in a long time." We start looking at them and see that there are holes in the production. The production could've been done a different way, and that's all detrimental to their case.

Ron: Are they're trying to save their clients' money by only bringing the experts in when they have to? Or do they just not believe they need the expert at that point, the litigators know enough?

Jorge: I think it's a combination of both. In some cases, they believe that they know enough that they've seen other complaints; they have other people who have worked on complaints that, I guess most of the discussion is in the audit malpractice area. So that they've seen it and they can file a complaint and that the case is going to settle.

Once they realize it's not going to settle, that now they know that these words that they have put into the complaint - any standards that are there - they know them. And maybe they know them on the intellectual level, but they haven't really lived them. They realize that now they need an expert.

But they're also trying to save their client's money. They're like "we're going to take this case; we're going to be very efficient. We're going to try to settle it right away." And a lot of times it doesn't work out that way.

Ron: Could there be drawbacks to bringing the experts in too early?

Jorge: Just the expense of bringing the expert in early. There's times where the expert is brought in early and says, "there's no case here. There's nothing." In that case, maybe the expert spent a few hours having a discussion with the lawyer and the client. And it turns out that there's a lot of money saved because they haven't gone through this long drawn out matter to find out that there's nothing here.

Ron: Say you're retained by litigators, you've been working on the case; how do they strategize with you? Or do they tell you what the strategy is and just have you buy in?

Jorge: It depends. Some firms really want you involved in almost every step of the way. They want you to help them put together deposition outlines and get involved in a lot of different aspects of the case. There are others where it's a very discreet thing that they want you to look at.

They basically give you their overall goal - we don't want our client to pay any fines. We want the investigation to go away. But they only provide a very discreet set of documents. They don't tell you the whole story of what happened, and you're very isolated from the overall strategy. You've been given just one piece of pie and that's all they want you to look at.

So it goes both ways. It depends on the lawyer and the sort of case that you've been given to work on.

Ron: If you disagree strongly with their strategy, do you voice that but always defer to them in the end?

Jorge: I definitely voice it. Because I know that if I don't voice it, in the end, I'm going to have to defend it. And it's a lot better to take care of it upfront and say, look, there's no way that anyone including myself with a straight face can say to someone that this is what happened or this is the value in damages.

But I will also work with them to think about a creative way that is supportable in the end. But it's going to have some basis in reality and it's got to be supportable. If we can work on that together, that's the perfect thing.

I understand that they want to win, I want to win. But it's got to be in a way where I'm not going to be hung out to dry and then eventually lose the case for them because I didn't believe in what they were saying.

Sometimes they'll be able to convince me that their approach is right. But I need to be able to do the work so that I can get to that point where I agree with them because I have a rational supportable basis to give my opinion.

Ron: Do they ask you to help them with discovery, with document requests?

Jorge: Yes. Not in every instance, but in a lot of instances, they do. In every case that we work on, we're requesting financial information. And you know what background, we have controllers, CFO's, and people in public accounting. There's no one more equipped to be able to say we need these sort of financial documents, we need these financial statements. The lawyers can send the other side an email saying, "hey, I'm looking for document requests related to X, Y and Z." But that's not the same as having a financial expert say you need X, Y and Z and be able to write it down in a way where the other side won't say, "oh, these guys don't know what they're talking about."

Ron: Let's say you're writing an expert report. Is it easier to write a rebuttal report or the initial expert report?

Which do you prefer if either?

Jorge: I prefer to write from scratch. But the rebuttal report is fun because initially, and this happens in every case that I work on, whether it's reading the other side's motion to dismiss or reading the rebuttal report; I read it for the first time and I'm horrified.

Then when I start getting into the very granular sort of things and start getting little openings and you start to unravel their theory. Once you start, generally, there's an overriding theme. Once you get in there and show that the overriding theme is not a legitimate theory, then the whole thing starts falling apart.

For me, putting the pieces together is more fun than writing the rebuttal.

At first, I'm reading a report and I'm like, oh. And then, once you start going through and analyzing each of the sections of the expert report; you're like, oh, it doesn't really make sense and then that doesn't make sense. Then all of a sudden, you're able to find a lot of flaws.

Ron: Are you commonly asked for previous reports you've issued before you're retained?

Jorge: You know, it's funny, no.

Attorneys don't much worry about that because, generally, they feel that whatever it is they're going to be able to fix the writing anyway.

They just want the report and they're looking at the credentials. It's a bonus and it's what probably gets you retained a second time to be able to write a report where the lawyer doesn't have to put in a lot of time. But I haven't had them. I think that's the reason that they're like, it's great if he writes, fantastic. But if it's a mess, we have whatever amount of associates that can go in and clean it up, I think. I think that's why.

Ron: Have you ever tracked down an opposing expert's previously issued report or somebody whose previously worked with them or against them - a litigator?

Jorge: No. I've been able to find an opposing expert's chapter in a book in connection with the same subject area that he was being deposed in.

The lawyers weren't aware of this. I found the book, copied the pages, and sent the pages to them before their deposition so that they could use that to depose him.

Ron: Did they love that?

Jorge: Yes, that's a perfect example of getting somebody involved in other aspects of the case. Where we're going to depose him, can you put together questions? Not only did I get their bio but I also sent them the book.

Ron: This is a perfect lead into my next two questions. One is about being prepared for your testimony - how the lawyers work with you - and then also, helping prepare the lawyer for deposing the opposing experts. First, please take me though how they prepare you for your deposition testimony and also the cross examination if you're going to be testifying in a trial.

Jorge: Some attorneys are very methodical; they'll take the expert report and go line by line. They'll ask you about the questions and help you refine your answers. Those are the ones I like to work with because I feel that they are on top of it and that they will protect me in a deposition or the trial.

Ron: They'll protect you because you're well prepared?

Jorge: Right.

           They'll protect me because they're being proactive. They're not like, "oh, just go out there and give it your best shot."

           Then there's the other attorneys who will call you up and say you're going to get deposed in a few days. You'll meet with them for an hour or two and it will be fairly loose. Those worry me a lot because I don't know if they've thought about the strategy or if they've thought about how I fit into their overall strategy.

           If they're not looking to me to be able to explain certain things like they said to me, "look, you're going to be deposed for x amount of time. We really want you to make this point or we really want you to focus on this part of the report." But not all attorneys are so thorough in their preparation.

Ron: As far as the opposing experts, does your side want your input on the depositions, the questions for the opposing expert; do they want you there at the deposition?

Jorge: Sometimes they want you there, but the other side won't agree to it. But the ones that I've worked with, at a minimum, want questions drafted; any sort of research that I can come up like have they written any articles or any books or do you have any thoughts on any of that sort of information that's available out there and to help them prepare in that way. Not every litigator is going to ask for that, but I think it adds a lot of value to be able to say these are the things you should be looking for; these are the things he is going to say, which is good practice.

Ron: Are you sometimes surprised when you read an opposing expert's report that it has typos or grammatical errors or it's so off point? Do you see that?

Jorge: I do see that. What surprises me the most from the expert reports I've seen and this is, as a litigator, that you get this report that is almost written like a college paper or something where it's just a rambling sort of a long document and you can't figure out what the point is. And excluding the typographical errors, it's more about the substance and organization of the report where it's very hard to figure out what the whole point of the document is.

Obviously, the typographical errors do not belong there, but the organization and substance of the reports really surprises me that they get issued like that.

Ron: I have one more question. And then if there's anything else you want to add, keeping in mind this book is about how litigators win their financial disputes by using their financial experts. As a financial expert, will you tell us a story about one time where you were involved in a case that you helped? That your side won because of the strategy you provided as a financial expert.

Jorge: There was a recent case; it was an arbitration and there were not a lot of documents. There were agreements that were not complete.

Ron: What type of agreement? Is it a purchase agreement?

Jorge: Purchase. There was a purchase agreement and there was an operating agreement as well as some deal agreements. Our client had entered into an asset purchase agreement with another individual. The other individual had expressed to him that he would be the financial guy and our client would be the face of the business. He would be the one that runs the business, does the marketing and all that. Our client is not a financial person and he was thrilled that this was going to happen.

We got involved in the case fairly late. We asked for documents, but they really couldn't get them to us.

Ron: What does that mean "they really couldn't get them to you"?

Jorge: Because the documents were lost.

Ron: They were purposely lost?

Jorge: The former partner of our client basically took them and probably destroyed them.

I helped them with their briefs to the arbitrator. When the arbitration started, I helped them with questions for the witnesses. But beyond that, it was impossible to put together a report with bits of information to come up with a damages calculation based on solid grounds.

Ron: So, are you making reasonable assumptions?

Jorge: They were reasonable assumptions. In this case, the parties in one of their agreements had stated that the partner, the defendant, was going to put in $8 million for 25% of the business. When you applied a 20% discount, that gives it a $40 million value. So we used that for $40 million value pointing to these agreements.

During the testimony, I was able to explain to the arbitrator that the other side was claiming that the asset purchase agreement was only for $100,000. And the defendants were asserting that that was the agreement and that the other monies that were provided to our client were loans. I was able to convince the arbitrator that it was not only the asset purchase agreement, but that there were other agreements that made the whole deal come in to play. And that was a deal points that was initialed and signed.

Although it wasn't a formal contract, it was the best agreement they had in place and the arbitrator agreed with me that that was the operative agreement. And that, based on the value agreed to by the parties, was $40 million.

Through that whole process, I helped them and looked over their briefs. I helped them during the arbitration with questions for the different witnesses and I eventually testified. With those questions, we were successful in the case. But that was the case where it seemed like there was nothing there when we first started, and I don't think that the litigators had any idea that the damages were going to be $40 million.

Ron: And the arbitrator agreed that that what's the defendants owed, $40 million?

Jorge: Exactly. $40 million plus punitive damages, I think the result was something like $50 million.

Ron: If the client had said six months earlier, we'll settle with you for $5 million; would they have taken that?

Jorge: Probably. They would have probably settled for $5 million.

Ron: Did the defendants think they owed $5 million?

Jorge: No. The defendants were very arrogant and thought that they were clever in that the documents didn't support any sort of claim.

Ron: So, they were pretty convinced they would owe zero?

Jorge: That they would owe zero and that, in fact, they were owed money for the funds that they had forwarded.

Ron: So, this was a super success.

That's a fantastic story with a fantastic ending for your client.

CHAPTER 2

LAWRENCE CARNEVALE

Ron: How do you determine where to find your experts?

Lawrence: There are a variety of sources available online. Many groups that are available to identify and make available experts, in particular areas. The greatest tool that I use is referrals from other lawyers who have been successful in utilizing financial experts. Outside the area of econometric analysis - that is primarily the area of forensic accounting and certain lost profits calculations - it is very important to find experts that can communicate well particularly if the case involves a jury trial.

Résumés are important and are often available online. But the actual performance of the people and their ability to relate to juries is really the litmus that we should all consider.

Ron: And when you said "communicate", do you mean verbally or written or both?

Lawrence: I'm saying primarily, verbally. The written material has to make sense as well. Most often in a trial or an arbitration, the actual report while reviewed by your adversary is not something that goes into the hands of the finder of fact. That's because the document itself is not evidence; what is evidence is the testimony of the witness.

It normally will contain demonstrative proof that the fact finder will see from time to time. The key issue is their ability to communicate moderately complicated facts in a simple and direct fashion. And then also to be able to think quickly and clearly on their feet and respond to challenging cross-examination.

Ron: What are the areas of specialty you believe are appropriate for a financial expert?

Lawrence: In any instance in which there is valuation matter or where there is some question of lost profits or financial injury, financial experts are often essential. They are particularly essential when there are circumstances when the calculation has to be made as to injury over a future period of time because that requires a number of assumptions. In other words, if you're going to make an assessment or analysis of lawsuits to occur over a future period, you always have to make certain assumptions which are accepted as a matter of financial convention and/or the appropriate accounting principles.

If the injury has already occurred, you may not necessarily need an expert because it may be on the books and records of the company and something that can be explained by a Chief Financial Officer or someone at the company. The primary value of experts is trying to understand as yet incurred but likely to incur injury.

Ron: What are the qualifications you seek in your financial experts?

Lawrence: Certainly, education is important, experience is important. That is a résumé that demonstrates that the expert has in fact successfully offered testimony. And when I say successful, I don't necessarily mean successfully in terms of delivering an outcome but having been allowed to testify by a court. Under both State and Federal principles, experts before they testify, can be challenged.

The well-known case from the federal courts is the Daubert case which deals with what type of evidence will be considered by the courts. You want to make sure you pick someone who has not been viewed by the court, in any court, as incompetent or a person that is incompetent to provide the testimony sought.

There are a number of things that can come into play. This is why it's very important for experts to be cautious about what assignments they take on because you could be a perfectly suitable candidate to offer expert testimony of a certain type in a certain case. But if asked to address certain subjects that are not either within the wheelhouse of that particular expert or situations where it would be irresponsible to offer an opinion, an expert can get into trouble. It's great to be entrepreneurial but an expert always has to be mindful that they are being used in a way in which the lawyer and the expert are confident that their expertise comes to sides with the scope of the testimony that's going to be offered.

Ron: Would you ever use an expert that's never testified before but seems to be credible to you and has the experience?

Lawrence: This is obviously an issue that comes up from time to time particularly in areas where the expertise is very limited, where there are not many people that you have as options. That tends not to be the case for instances in standard forensic accounting, there are plenty of folks that are capable in that area.

The simple answer is there are circumstances where I would and that could depend on a number of things. If the education is right; if after meeting the expert, I am satisfied that they have good verbal skills we're able to formulate responses in an efficient and direct way. And that I was satisfied that they understood the law and the facts of the given circumstance, it might make sense. An advantage of a witness who has never testified before is that there is no prior testimony to impeach him with so he or she comes a tabula rasa.

The downside is that lack of testimonial experience is often emphasized by your adversary to the fact finder as an indication that perhaps the expert doesn't have qualifications or equivalent qualifications to the competing expert.

Ron: Do you prefer an academic versus a practicing accounting versus somebody who is a professional expert witness?

Lawrence: It's interesting. In the area of econometric analysis would be testimony modeling what an economic environment would look like but for certain past events. These guys often testify in any trust litigation and sometimes with regard to the situation such as the causes for stock market movements or indications.

In my experience, those folks are always academics, and almost always are also at the same time, people who testify. There is no actual practice other than, as I understand it, for those folks other than theoretical.

Of course for practicing accountants, I have had great success with folks who are CPAs. I wouldn't exclude someone who is an accountant or a forensic accountant because he or she is also an academic. That can certainly be an advantage because it's an amplification item for their résumé. But I think the most practical experience and the more testimonial experience a person has, the more likely he or she is to be user-friendly both with the lawyer preparing the testimony and also in communicating with the jury or the fact finder.

Ron: Do you inquire or does it matter how many times an expert has been on the plaintiff side or the defendant side?

Lawrence: There are certain litigations where that's important. For example, in certain forms of contractual disputes, insurance, in particular, you would not ordinarily want to use experts who have testified on both sides of an issue, because they can be challenged. Typically, where there are contractual provisions, the history of the development of legislations or things like that come up, you want somebody that has been consistent in testifying. That often tracks whether they are supporting a plaintiff position or not.

For example, in the insurance industry, historically in the environmental dispute field, there are certain experts brought in to recite the history of the development of environmental coverage under hazard provisions in various policies. You can imagine that the person who's going to want to use those folks is someone trying to gain insurance and who's being told that they can't have it by the insurance company.

The interpretation very often is going to follow whether they are plaintiff's person or not. There are certain instances, however, where that's not true. In forensic accounting, it really doesn't matter because you may be asked to assess whether or not someone's assumptions about future projections make sense or not. And so the fact that they may have testified for a defendant in rejecting what may appear to be inflated projections of a plaintiff's expert, I'd have no problem using them on either side of the case.

You have to look at each situation to know whether they're likely competent to or they would be effective as an expert on the opposite side of the case and keep it. One thing that we absolutely can't do is have an expert contradict him or herself with respect to the same subject matter which can happen if he or she is on the opposite side of the case.

Ron: What are some essential traits and characteristics that you identify in a financial expert?

Lawrence: I need to be able to communicate with the expert. That means when they speak, there's always a disconnect, an imbalance in expertise between the lawyer and the accountant with regard to accountancy just as there is an imbalance favoring the lawyer in terms of the law. Because the presentation of the evidence at trial on financial issues is governed by legal principles, lawyers and accountants have to communicate clearly in the legal principles within which the financial testimony is offered.

What that requires is a good and clear communication between the financial expert and the lawyer. Just hiring the expert and telling him to do the work and not reviewing or carefully interacting with him or her over time can be disastrous. Without guidance, an accountant may perfectly well apply general accounting principles, appropriate modeling for certain concepts. But those concepts are not ones recognized as appropriate for the court. One dynamic or tension that always exists when lawyers work with accountants is the accountants might have the tendency to want to create financial projections that to me look and smell like valuation models. They're basically business valuation.

Business valuation and projection of lost profits have similarities because they often involve looking into the future, revenue streams, future expenses, issues of interest rates, all kinds of things that would affect the profitability of the business going forward. But, for example, in a lost profit scenario, you need to understand very clearly what time period you're projecting the loss over.

From the valuation standpoint, a forensic accountant or valuation person would use the discounted cash flow analysis, whatever that would be. Normally, when it's a 7, 8 or 9- year projection period and a discount back is what their instinct would be. It's not an irrational approach, but it's not necessary. Let's say, for example, the contracting question only covers a period of 4 years or let us say for example the only rational way in which one can look at the damages scenario is not over 10 years but over a shorter period of time.

Experts and lawyers need to communicate. It's critical that you have an open and clear communication with the expert and the expert is willing to accept guidance of that type. In that way, the testimony will coincide with the basic legal principles governing it. My number 1 is that.

Number 2, they have to be articulate but not officious. As an expert, you need to be able to say what you mean in the simplest and clearest of terms. At the risk of sounding negative, it's a bit of the lowest common denominator effect. The accountant is always going to know numerous times the level of information about the subject matter than any fact finder whether it would be a judge or a jury or an arbitration panel. And yet, despite the fact that these are things that many people don't deal with on a regular basis. She's going to have to communicate this information in a way that is understandable. This is both a language matter and it is also a question that I find that the best experts are the ones that can find a graphic representation of what they're saying that's effective.

We all know that accountants can generate reams of spreadsheets. Spreadsheets are not generally effective as an argumentative tool before a fact finder. They are dense. You need to think about graphics as a means of communication. Again, communication with the lawyer is key, communication skills and the ability to distill and articulate in the simplest possible terms.

The last critical element has to be that they need to be facile in responding to cross-examination. This is not simply a situation where they need to deny everything that a cross-examiner may ask them. They need to be able to think through the issue. But a belligerent expert, one who just simply sticks by his guns and is not prepared to work through the issue with a cross-examining expert is not always ideal.

The hardest thing that experts have to go through, financial expert or others, is the cross- examination process. And that's for two reasons. The first thing is that the person asking the questions has no interest in supporting the expert's view. Their entire mission is to dissemble it. The second thing is the questioner is not as experienced as the witness so there's always a big risk of miscommunication. An expert hearing something that sounds like one thing to an accountant but means something else to other people.

The best experts are ones that don't simply say "no" every time a cross-examination is done with them, but actually try to field and explain why whatever assumption they're being asked to make or whatever assumption that's being challenged in support of them.

Ron: Do your experts commonly use demonstratives?

Lawrence: Yes, in every case I will insist on it.

Ron: What are some core skills you identify your experts need to possess?

Lawrence: There are the three things we talked about and the last thing is we need time. We need that time available to prepare. The largest mistake that most lawyers make is not trying to comprehend their expert. They just leave the expert. It's tempting for a lawyer to do that because the lawyer can recognize he'll never fully understand what his expert is doing. But it's a mistake.

The expert needs time to spend. And what do I mean by that? I'm talking about preparation where you sit down with the lawyer and go over what the testimony will be - what the questions are. When I ask the questions, what am I actually asking for? Recall, that in trials generally, the lawyers can't ask leading questions with their own witnesses. I can't ask an expert, "Isn't it true, Sir, that the damages, in this case, are $100 million?" No. I have to ask a question, "did you render an opinion?" "What is your opinion?" "Can you tell us the assumptions that underlay it?" They need to understand and be organized in their response.

Organization is probably the biggest skill that an expert in financial matters needs to bring because there are many layers of what they do. First, they gather the information. And second, they digest it. They apply assumptions to it and then provide their conclusions as a result of it. Each step of the way they need to be able to explain what those elements are.

The skill of organization is critical. Practicing the skill of explaining organization and understanding how to explain is important. When I say, what assumptions did you rely on, you need to be able to say "I applied the following four fundamental assumptions. I applied this discount rate. I applied it over this period of time and I did it for this reason in the following area." And as a result of applying those assumptions to the evidence that you had from the financial records of the company what were you able to conclude? "The following...."

So, organization is in addition to good oral skills.

Ron: When have you seen a forensic accountant be ineffective either on your side or the other, what are some of the reasons for that ineffectiveness?

Lawrence: Lack of preparation, lack of care in listening to the question are the major two. When I say preparation, most experts are pretty good at being able to explain what they did. They're not always so good in understanding all of the facts of the case that might influence whether the assumptions that they use are appropriate. But this is critical because you don't get away with being able to avoid the sensibility or the actual factual support for an assumption just because you're a financial expert. And this is one thing where for example, the financial expert;

"Over what period of time did you project losses?"

"Over 4 years."

"And why did you choose that period?"

"Well, the client told me to. They feel that's the right duration."

"Well, why did they feel that way?"

"I don't know."

"Do you have any independent opinions as to whether that 4-year period is appropriate?"

"I don't know."

You see that's the problem. Okay, as compared to;

"Over what period did you do the analysis?"

"4 years"

"Why?"

"Well, because after having a look at the data and having discussed it with the client we concluded that the average durability of an account of this type is 4 years. And so the loss of accounts of this type can be reasonably resolved in damages over a 4-year period."

"And how do you know that?"

"Well, I reviewed the facts in the case. We did a study of the company's books and records going back 8 years and found that this is the average lifetime of an account."

That's preparation. That's what you need to be able to do to fend off a successful cross- examination. That is the one thing that takes a lot of time and it's the one thing that many experts don't do. And it's probably mostly not their fault. It's the lawyer's fault for not having provided them with that. And that often comes from a lack of communication.

Ron: When do you retain your experts?

Lawrence: At the outset of the case. If I am plaintiff, I may very well hire a financial expert before I even initiate a case. Unless the case has to be initiated on an emergent basis like seeking a restraining order or an injunction for trade secret or something like that. Where damages are going to be a serious factor, or if any client is trying to decide whether or not to pursue litigation, I like to bring in an expert then. We should retain an expert at the earliest possible moment so that he or she can make appropriate valuations or assessment as to what investments should be made in the case whether in fact damages are provable. There are many instances in which damages are very difficult to establish with any certainty.

Yes, I would always, as a plaintiff, bring on an expert as early as possible. If I don't need to file an emergent pleading, I would hire them before I even file my complaint so that I have a good sense of the value of what it's about that I'm about to initiate. It is absolutely bad practice to just file a case with a large claim for damages where you have no realistic basis; although lawyers do this frequently. The embarrassment that comes later is if you just throw a number into a pleading that you think you might be able to prove and your expert comes in ten times that or one-tenth of that. Whatever you said in the beginning of the case stands because you never thought to check with an expert. And then your adversary will likely say, "Well didn't you say when you filed this case that damages were X?"

If you are a defendant, your early analysis is important because you need to understand it from the standpoint of the settlement matrix. If you're looking at the situation, put aside liability for a moment, where if liability is established because damages are pretty easy to establish; your guy should be able to advise you of that soon. Responsible lawyers should get experts involved at the earliest stage. The latest possible time they can get involved is at a point in time in which expert reports are being exchanged.

Ron: Are there any drawbacks to bringing in your expert during the pleading stage rather than later?

Lawrence: I can't think of one.

Ron: I have a couple of questions on strategizing with your experts. You alluded to earlier how you like to prepare them. Do you strategize with them on how you see the case moving?

Lawrence: I think you always have to. Each forensic expert will have often more than one way of approaching the problem. And there may be one way or another way to present different strengths of assumptions underlying the report. Your goal should be to find the strongest report. If there is more than one theory of damages available or methodologies to reach a damage analysis, then the strategy is to decipher or decide which of those provides the least exposure to cross-examination.

One thing that I often do, which is not unique, but is the subject of constant debate among practitioners is whether to offer alternative damage theories or subsets of laws. There is a strategy there as well. It is more common than not that if I meet with a forensic expert; they will favor giving me a number, the number is X. But let's say I'm projecting loss over four years and there are strong arguments for that but perhaps there are strong arguments as well for a two-year period. I could simply come in with my expert and say, boom, "four years, $81 million." Or, I could come in with a report that shows the evolution of loss over a period of time.

My expert could come in and say damages are accruing over a period of four years in this way. So after four years the injury is X and that's what I believe the injury is. But if I was asked to analyze what injury accrued as at two years, the number would be X. What I do there is I hedge my bet. Maybe I have a judge that is uncomfortable with a four-year period; maybe I have almost equally strong reasons for applying a certain assumption.

There is a strategy and a technique designed to hedge. Putting too many alternatives out there creates the appearance of indecision and disorganization. You have to be very careful when you offer alternatives. Sometimes you can offer as an alternative a test theory in which you make your calculation under one methodology. Then you apply a different methodology just to see whether it comes in within the same ballpark. And the testimony suddenly is, "Here's the damage. And just in case if you wanted to know, we tested it under another theory and came out very close. I'm not saying our damage theory is that, but even if you are to use a different methodology, you will find a damage number yielded very similar in dimensions and scale to the one that I'm reporting."

The strategy is obviously critical. And again, this is a question of communication. It also is a question of how comfortable the expert is with certain assumptions that may underlie things. Lawyers may feel very comfortable with an assumption that an expert won't feel comfortable with. It's a two-way street in that discussion. The strategy is to take a look at the case and take a look at where the likely cross-examination is going to come. Assess the best way to rebut that and then choose among alternatives which have the least vulnerability to that analysis.

I'm a big fan of showing, in any kind of projection, of loss over time, how loss evolves over time. In case someone has a different idea, including the jury, how long the damages period should be. Probably the biggest issue for forensic accountants are lost profits damages. No one tells you. There isn't a contract that tells you over what period of time you're going project loss. Lawyers argue about this every day in every courtroom in every state in the country. And it's never going to go away. It's a constant battle. The reason is the law says, as a rule generally, damages don't have to be established to a scientific certainty but they must not be speculative. These words sound important. But when you actually try to understand what you're being told in that regard, it's not so easy to understand. Not scientific but not speculative.

We're constantly challenging ourselves to understand where we might be challenged as to potentially speculative or irresponsible projections.

Ron: When you're developing your discovery requests, do you use financial experts?

Lawrence: We try to.

If I'm looking for financial data, it would make sense to get your expert in - what does he need from the other side to understand? In every financial analysis, you have two methods or two potential methods to examine. Either what were the profits gained by your adversary or the bad person as a result of their conduct? That means looking in their files or what did you lose by looking in your files. For example, you would look and see, well do I see a diminution or a decline in revenue? That's one way of measuring it.

Other ways of looking at things like these would be to say, well, if this person had been producing revenue for me, then the revenue would have looked like this. That would be an analysis where I'd project whatever that person had been doing over time going forward. And when he left, you could either say he left and so there was the difference between where he was and where the company ended up. Or you might say the difference is something about where he would have been versus where the company ended up. And they may be different numbers.

I think that addresses it.

The expert has to be very careful in asking the client that he represents what he needs and make sure he's getting reliable data from some source. And that he understands the data that he's getting so that his projections make sense when they're all done. The second side is asking for information from the other side and that may be for a variety of reasons. Even if you don't want to make your damage model based on what information you get from the other side.

What the other side's information shows may be a test against your theories on your own. It's not always necessarily a zero-sum analysis. In other words, some business or group of people conducting a business could move to a competitor, for example, but the environment there is not the same as it was because of the client mix or other things. Their performance might not be a perfect proxy for what they might have been able to perform had they stayed with you.

You absolutely need your expert to help make sure you obtain what data you need and in what form you need it in. And very often, the ideal form to get is a manipulable form. It's something where you can't change the numbers, but you can move them around. A lot of lawyers fail to do that and they end up costing their clients a ton of money because the experts have to input them all in a program which is a time-consuming process.

Ron: Do you ask potential experts for previously issued reports?

Lawrence: Almost all the courts require in the expert report a list of prior testimony. And usually, that's where we would start. If the testimony is available, we would look at it at least in respect of cases of the same type that we're talking about here. It's a good idea that the expert retains that himself because that makes it simpler for everybody. Often that's not the case and the hunt for the record is tricky. But if you can, and if it's available, a smart lawyer will always do that.

Ron: And you said earlier that the reports probably are not entered into evidence.

So you have to get them from the other side. They're not public so...

Lawrence: That is true, generally. They're not going to be found in the court's annals unless there's some challenge to the report and there was some motion that the testimony should be barred because the report is flawed. But yes, that's exactly right. So testimony is key.

Ron: When you read an expert report, what have you found to be the most compelling aspects of those reports?

Lawrence: There, it's always a question of organization, too. And not one size fits all for every case. The more complex the facts, the more moving parts there are, it may change how you want to present the material. But the organization is critical. Normally, your report should provide some kind of expert summary or executive summary in the beginning, saying where you're going. Much of the organization of expert reports is guided statutorily. The federal rules of evidence tell you basically what the report has to look like. It has to give certain data about the expert. It has to say what his opinions are and his reasons for them, things like that.

Broadly speaking, there isn't a lot of flexibility in an expert report because you're following statutory or procedural requirements. But, within that construct, obviously, there are ways. You could provide a report that doesn't have an executive summary and just has some long presentation and at the very end, there's a number with a big double marked line under it that says "damages."

Typically, we prefer less verbiage and more accounting and critical analysis. In other words, there'd be an executive summary; there would be a very simple statement of the types of the damages analysis that are going on. But the real guts of the thing will be in the exhibits attached to it, which are the spreadsheets that would be applied, that show the underlying data.

Organization is the key. If a judge is going to look at it, he will probably be the only person that will see an expert report and probably only if there's a challenge. If he reads it and can't comprehend it in any way, that's a problem. So, it should have some organization to it.

Ron: My next question, I think you answered earlier. When you're preparing your experts for testimony, preparing them for direct and for cross, you said preparation is key. How do you prepare them?

Lawrence: I would sit down and have to be a lengthy discussion with the expert. It would be a frank discussion with the expert about what he sees or what he'd expect the vulnerabilities are in his report. That's not a sign of weakness. Every expert should understand which of the assumptions that he relies on are the soundest and which are the farthest out on the speculation meter.

Once the lawyer has a good sense of what the expert is trying to do, we sit him down in a room and cross-examine him. We see how facile they are in explaining the facts.

An example question might be, "Mr. Rosenfarb, isn't it a fact that your assumption is based strictly on hearsay from some analyst's report on Citibank? And why do you think that analyst is any kind of authority with respect of X?"

If that's true, the expert needs to understand, "Well, Citi's been covering that client for 35 years. They have a singularly most well-respected analyst on earth and he's been right in projecting the target's price for that stock for the last 35 years. He's a pretty good analyst and we thought about that. There are eight other analysts that cover that company, but not one of them are at the same level of respect or accuracy of this fellow."

They need to understand those kinds of things. So, we would mock-cross them.

Ron: What about when you're getting ready to depose the opposing expert?

Lawrence: We always consult our expert before that and often bring them to the deposition if it's allowed.

And that is for the obvious reason that experts are going to hear things that the lawyer doesn't hear. Very often an expert will say something in a way that another expert knows is just fudging. So you need to know that. It's very dangerous not to bring your financial expert to the deposition of the other person. And it's a routine practice.

Ron: Will you share with us a story about when you used an expert when it went well or when it didn't?

Lawrence: As a young lawyer, I hired a very respected accounting firm. Then, it was one of the big six. They were very expensive and very thorough. But their procedure was, in my view, unusual that to this day I don't entirely understand it. The report and the analysis were prepared by a group within the accounting firm. The testifying expert did not prepare, he was just the mouthpiece.

There were vetting processes in which he was allowed to participate after the fact. But I forget how or why this accounting firm felt this was the best way to present this. But what I didn't realize was that the people that I was working through the whole matter with all the time and that the interaction and the development of the expert report was with a group from the accounting firm, other than the potential testifying expert. While they were very well-versed in all of the issues, what I failed to appreciate was that their ability to communicate my thoughts to the testifying expert was limited. So what they felt, I think, was, they didn't want to expose their expert to the argument of preparation by counsel so that it didn't appear as though lawyers were sticking words in the expert's mouth, right?

So that testifier would never have to say, "Did you talk to the lawyer on the other side?"

"No. No."

Or, "Have you met me before?"

"Yes."

"And when did we talk?"

"We talked at the outside of this retention and we talked on the way in here."

"Did I tell you what you were supposed to say here today?"

He said, "No."

And that was, I think, the goal that they were trying to accomplish which was to create the appearance that what the jury or the judge was getting was a fresh and unadulterated and uncoached questioning. This is sort of a silly concept since obviously everything is coached.

But what happened was that testifying expert, not having been allowed to work with me directly, beforehand, when I asked him questions he struggled to understand precisely what I was asking. He also didn't seem to have a firm grasp on some of the issues that I had discussed extensively with his staff.

From that moment forward, any major accounting firm that says to me that they have to separate their testifying expert from the worker bees who put it together, I would never consider retaining. I don't care if someone challenges my expert because he met with me to discuss this. I will characterize that as responsible preparation.

On the bright side, the other issue that you have with experts is, again, communication skills. I have hired, in the past, people whose résumés were astounding, but simply don't speak English. And this isn't good either. I need my expert to have the unique ability to communicate and to respond to challenges in a manner where he doesn't get flustered. And hopefully, he enjoys the challenge of thinking through the questions and is extremely alert.

Also, my expert should be very active throughout the entire process. Although he likely doesn't run the analyses, he's very active in the process nonetheless.

This is critical. You must be in constant contact with the testifying person. He needs to understand you. You need to have a rapport with him. When you get him on the stand, he needs to understand why and what you're going to ask him. The bad situations have always been ones in which the expert was not a good communicator or the expert was not properly prepared. The only time that ever happened to me was when I wasn't given the opportunity to prepare him. And that will never happen again.

Ron: My last question is - do you find it common in young associates that they don't know how to use financial experts or when to retain them and what cases to bring them in on?

Lawrence: I think lawyers, as a rule, don't understand accounting principles and they can't read a balance sheet or a financial statement. I know I even struggle with it. And I have been taught over and over again by many different forensic accountants. I think I know what a lot of the words mean now and I think I know why things are set up.

But one critical thing, for all the young lawyers, is that there should be some bare-bones course for any lawyer in a commercial law firm about how to read a balance sheet and a financial statement. Young lawyers need a basic understanding of how financial documents work. You can't even get to the point of thinking about an expert, retaining an expert, interviewing an expert, vetting one or anything else unless you can begin to understand basic financial principles.

There are always going to be some young people who studied accounting in college or someone who has intrinsic and already existing expertise. Obviously, they're a good person to have on your case if you're going to be seeking damages. But it's critical that on any serious case, for the expert work to be done with a relatively senior person at the lawyer level. Why is that? Number one, you need the experience to understand the problems that experts can get into. There are so many things that go into picking and vetting the expert which is very practical. You're looking for indicia that you think are going to be something that defines a good expert and a competent testifier.

I think it's a mistake to put expert's selection and preparation in the hands of junior lawyers. It's hard enough to put on lay testimony at trial because of the unusual way in which personalities work. I mean witnesses will forget or witnesses will misrecollect or not understand the question and say something odd, even if you've prepared them. That is transported and multiplied by ten when you're dealing with an expert because your best hope as a lawyer is to understand about 10% of what they do. You need to know enough so that you know how to cue them.

Some of the largest law firms in town have specialist lawyers that deal with experts in major cases. They would never put on a lay witness, they would never write a brief, but their specialty is effectively communicating financial principles. That is less common among most law firms out there, but it is illustrative of the fact that this is something everyone recognizes is a specialty and a skill. It's because of the expertise differential between the lawyers and the accountants and takes a lot of work. Even if you've done it a hundred times, it takes a lot of work to make sure you and the expert are talking about the same thing.

Ron: I want to open it up in case there's something else you want to talk about, anything you want to bring up.

Lawrence: The actual process of preparing and presenting expert testimony is not so mysterious. It's a lot of hard work and preparation. That's all there is. If you cheat on it or if you're looking your expert in the eye and can tell that he's having a hard time keeping a straight face doing what you're asking him to do, you need to be alert to this because he will get crushed on cross-examination if he's not comfortable with doing what he's asked to do.

There's no substitution for early communication, honest communication, frequent communication and preparation. And you just can't do enough with an expert. Every time you go through it, something will come up and you'll go, "Oh, really?" and you'll say, "Wow, that's a thought. I didn't even think of that before," because experts aren't memorizing a sentence or a word. When I prepare a witness, I'm not telling him what words to use. I may be telling him what concepts to emphasize or what I'm asking him to do.

It's very common that in preparation and examination when we're going over how the testimony will sound, a word will be used, his statement would be now, "Hey, you never said that before. What does that mean?" And then we'll find out that a fundamental component of this analysis is not what I thought. That's why this preparation and re-preparation process is critical because you can do it several times.

We have this example recently where we prepared the report three or four years ago. The case has been going on forever. And as we sought to come down the pipe to finally prepare the final report as it had become due last year; we realized that there were some things that we were talking about that we had not synchronized our thinking on. We were very happy to spot that before we filed the expert report and we fixed it. But, it scared me because if we had been rushing, I don't know. That's another reason why you don't want to wait till the last minute to hire an expert. You need time to let this stuff digest and distill.

CHAPTER **3**

HARVEY FEUERSTEIN & JOHN GOLDMAN

Ron: So first, if you would each introduce yourself, your name.

Harvey: I'm Harvey Feuerstein, 77 years old and am in my 47th year at Herrick, Feinstein. I started practicing law in 1963 with the law firm Becker, Ross and Stone. I began with litigation and after 3 years I was permitted to work on corporate matters as well. The combination of litigation and corporate caused me to develop an interest in doing what I call "business divorce" when partners owning a successful business no longer want to be partners. The question is, how do you unscramble the egg? Who is going to get the business and at what price and how to avoid damaging the goodwill of the business?

John: I'm John Goldman, also a partner at Herrick. I have been here since 1987 when I was a summer associate and have been coming to this building on Park Avenue ever since. I also do business divorce. There is quite a need in that context for experts in the field of business valuations.

Ron: Where do you determine to seek your experts?

Harvey: We have a roster of experts because we've had a lot of matters. Who we hire often depends upon the nature of the case. If it involves a particular profession or industry, we talk to people in that profession or industry about who are the leading valuation experts. When we go to trial, the jury and the judge want to hear from a witness expert in that profession or business, not some professor from Business School who may be brilliant but who doesn't have deep experience in that particular industry or profession.

John: I agree and would add that I often find the best experts who are not working on our side. There have been a number of instances over the years where we found some pretty good relationships in those types of situations.

The most important thing is that you have to know the situation that involves the fact-finding and expert testimony as well as getting a judge or a jury to believe what is being said by the expert. The expert is obviously knowledgeable, credible, presentable and understands how to get the point across. This is an important part of communication, not just about being right, but saying it the right way.

John: Sometimes experts don't understand that. We have to teach them.

Ron: What are the qualifications you seek in your financial experts?

Harvey: I look for an honest expert who is not going to blow smoke. He has an impressive résumé, has done this a number of times, is not frightened by a cross-examination and has a provenance and a pedigree.

We avoid blowhards and people who are just out to get a very good fee. I was in a case years ago where I was able to skewer the expert on the other side because he told a totally different story in the book that he published from the one he told on the stand.

John: As far as I know Sandy Koufax never did anything but pitch. In those days, I guess, he did hit. He was a really good pitcher. Some experts are really good at some things but not so good at others. You can have an expert who can write the best report but can't sit in a witness chair under cross-examination and do very well. The most important characteristic for the expert is what we use him for, who's our audience and what do we need them to do.

We need the best and often the group we use will have different people. They will have a pitcher, shortstop, catcher and right fielder. That helps because somebody will write a good report. However, the person they put up as their witness is the person who's able to give the right testimony. It is not always the person who authors the report, someone will do that for him.

When an expert makes a mistake and the mistake is highlighted during the trial on cross-examination, in my view, the expert's "toast." If a fact witness makes a mistake, they can sometimes recover from it. There is the theory that if you make one mistake or you lie once, you're prone to lie all the time.

I had an expert in a trial a year ago who made a careless mistake in preparing his report, but it was material. He didn't mean to make it, but he was dead the minute the fact finder saw that mistake.

What am I looking for? I look for somebody that is not going to make a mistake – careless or otherwise.

Harvey: How come your adversary didn't pick up the mistake?

John: I think the adversary didn't pick it up because they didn't read the report carefully enough and someone else did.

Harvey: That's the point of the story. That shouldn't have happened. He should've picked it up. Presumably, if John had had that guy as his expert, it wouldn't have happened.

He would have read the report very carefully. It's not only about being a bad expert; it is also bad lawyering.

Ron: Do you prefer an Academic, a professional expert witness?

Harvey: Every case is different. We are litigators. In the case that John took over, it had to do with the valuation of certain kinds of buildings in the city of New York. The expert is a guy in New York who's viewed as Joe DiMaggio in valuing that class of buildings. The best we could do was hire that man, not because he was necessarily the best, but because we knew our adversary thought he was Joe DiMaggio. Therefore, if that guy said this building was worth 3 million, 5 million or whatever it was, they were going to crumble.

John: I always want the same expert. Not the same person but the same sort of qualifications. I like to win. If I'm going to trial, I'm going to win. I need an expert to work with me and my team toward that goal. First and foremost, the expert has to have a certain level of skill and experience. I'm not the type who likes the expert who's testified in thousands of trials. Because they've testified in thousands of trials, that makes him a career expert witness, and that doesn't necessarily do me any good.

I want the person who will fit best into the audience that I have in a trial, and it could be the same person. Some people can do well in any environment. Other people are good in some circumstances, but not so good in others.

It really is the relationship that you have. The expert has to feel a part of the trial team. That is what caused the problem for that big international law firm we were against. The expert was alone and the lawyers were saying that, "We're the lawyers, you're just the expert." It can't be that way.

Ron: Do you ever find that you hear a judge really liked an expert and relies on their opinion?

Harvey: Absolutely, but sometimes it's just in the judge's demeanor or his face that lets you know whether your expert is carrying the day.

John: One of the questions to ask an expert when you know who your judge is going to be is if they have ever testified as an expert before this particular judge. It can't hurt to have someone who has done well before. When I say audience, that's what I'm talking about.

Who's my audience and how do I best approach that audience so that the communication of the facts and law gets heard?

Sometimes it's not what you say; it's how you say it. It's not a perfect system. Our system of jurisprudence is imperfect so we have to try to take the imperfections out of it. The best way to do that is to make sure that the communication flow is good. If the communication is faulty, it's going to cause problems.

Harvey: Before you hire an expert, you had better have cross-examined him or her very extensively. Sometimes they'll forget that they once handled a matter, you have to do your own independent research into their entire testimonial history. You have to become an expert on the expert.

Ron: Do you ask how many times they've been on the plaintiff side or the defense side?

John: Absolutely and I don't just trust what they say. It definitely matters to me. What can happen is that your expert has taken the opposite side of an issue and that comes up during cross-examination. Then his credibility is done; he's just a hired gun. America is a capitalistic society. Experts are paid to give their testimony. They are paid by the hour and by the matter. If they don't get the job, they don't get paid.

You have to make sure that doesn't become the issue.

Harvey: Experts want to publish in well-respected journals because it adds to their provenance and reputation.

John: And guys like us see them and say, "Ah, let's hire this guy...."

Harvey: This appeared in the Harvard Business Review. Now that is very impressive, right? The question is, what did he write in the Harvard Business Review and how does that relate to this case? Is it good or bad?

Ron: What are some core skills you identified in a forensic accountant?

Harvey: We've covered a good number of skills. The expert's ability to remain calm and cool under cross-examination and not get shaken or become doubtful when an adversary tries to rile him. But before that, thorough knowledge of what he's testifying about and consistency.

John: I'll also add one thing because you're asking about a specific type of professional expert, a forensic accountant, as opposed to a valuation expert.

A forensic accountant is somebody that will roll up his or her sleeves and get into the books and records of the bad guys and try to find things. That person is part of an effective team that needs to manage the expectations of the client and lawyers.

I want an expert, especially a forensic expert, who will do that analysis calmly and not get too crazy either way. Tell the truth, be honest, do a fair analysis and don't get nuts.

Harvey: The best thing he can do is not pontificate. In other words, he's not taking sides. He's just telling it like it is and like he knows it to be from many years of experience with such matters.

John: That is absolutely the best thing an expert can do. If he just is there, telling a story, a jury or even a judge will listen more carefully to what he says. If an academic gives explanations that nobody understands, they're going to sleep.

Ron: When you see an expert who is ineffective, whether on your side or your adversary, what are the reasons for that ineffectiveness?

John: It's just overcomplicating the issue. I like to keep things very simple. Effective communication is made in simple presentations. The worst thing an expert can do is sound like an expert.

Harvey:	The best litigator or trial lawyer is the one that can boil down massive amounts of facts to a simple message of why their client should win. And it follows that to be consistent find the expert who believes firmly in that simple message.
John:	Right. Think about your normal everyday life. Forget about being a lawyer or an expert and put yourself in the shoes of the every day juror who comes to court not wanting to be there. A lot of people say these people can't be smart because if they were smart they'd figure out a way to get out of jury duty, right?
	And judges who have hundreds of cases do not want to hear a legend that is the "same old, same old." They want something that entertains them, that keeps their attention, that interests them and that's easy to follow so that they can go home and tell their loved ones that "I had a really good time today."
	The highest compliment anybody ever paid me was at a jury trial in 2001, not long after 9/11. I walked into a restaurant less than two years ago, so more than 10 years later. One of the jurors was sitting at the bar turned around and said, "I know you. You were the lawyer in this case. I was on the jury." He said, "You were fantastic." The guy remembered me and spotted me after 10 years. I had made an impression on him. We didn't win. The jury split the baby and he was terrible for me.
Ron:	When do you hire your expert?
Harvey:	As soon as possible.
John:	Not necessarily. Unless you have an unlimited budget, which is never the case.
Harvey:	I'm talking about a case involving a valuation of a business in a business divorce. How much is this business worth? How much should my partner pay me if I agree to sell or to send them a letter that says I'll buy you at this price or you can buy me at that price?

That's a nice way of resolving a business divorce. It doesn't happen very often, but it's a very efficient way to do it. On the other hand, if it's a contract damage matter you'll have a consequential damages question – how much can I prove that my client suffered in damages? In such a case, hiring an expert won't be the immediate first thing I'm going to do.

John: If the assumption is that it is that business divorce type of a case then the valuation of the assets is critical and has to be done right away. In a case where you're looking at a breach of contract, a damage claim could be many millions of dollars. But you're not sure where the case is going to go. You have to prove liability before you get to damages. If your budget is limited or you're on a contingency, you may think about pushing that expense further down the road until you see where the case is going.

We're settling a claim now in a bankruptcy proceeding where we did not retain experts because we didn't want to pay for it. There might be instances where you wait a little bit. That's the real world for me.

Ron: Do you ever pick up the phone just to pick your expert's brain.

John: Absolutely. The nature of the relationship goes back to having people I can trust to give me an off-the-cuff, "Okay, this is where I think this is heading."

Ron: You said earlier that you want to make your experts feel like they're part of the team. How do you strategize with your experts and how do you do that?

John: I sit with them. I look at them and challenge their theories and cross-examine them on their thinking. I try to figure out what the real answer is even though they are the expert and I am the lay person so that I can simplify it and present it in a way that will be understood. In this way I can manage the expectations of the client. That's my job.

Harvey: John is correct. We always have to deal with the practical money issue because litigation is so expensive and whether or not the case can warrant it, whether the client can afford it and so on.

Sometimes you have a client that says there was a breach and now you're racking your brain to see how much damages you can collect. To prove a breach is one thing; to prove that you actually suffered damages is a very different exercise. Sometimes an expert can be very helpful in helping to frame things after doing an analysis of the business and financials. It could intimidate your adversary into sitting down and talking to you about settlement because he never thought about the elements of damage an expert creatively uncovers.

It depends again on the case. But, I've done that before to good effect.

Ron: Do you use your experts to draft your document requests for discovery?

John: I have not said, "Okay, you draft it." But I've certainly consulted with the experts in formulating the best approach when seeking documents from the other expert. I've also sat with experts for many hours and have had them sit-in on an expert depositions when possible, or do a mock deposition to figure out what we want to ask about the documents they produced to us. That's part of the team building thing that I like. They're involved, they're invested, they're part of the team and they're helping me with strategy. I don't like it when they complicate matters. That's when they get to be shoved off to the side. If they're helping me simplify it and get the answers I need in a deposition, absolutely.

Harvey: Of course. They're the ones who sometimes come up with a devastatingly poignant question that you can ask that could win the case.

John: Well, not only that. There are law firms and lawyers who are sharp in their practice so they will read a request quite literally. If you don't ask for the right thing, you won't get it. When it surfaces at trial, they're going to say, "You didn't ask for this and the expert will reply, "But I did." The expert can be very helpful in helping frame the request perfectly so that problem is avoided. That's how I use them in that context.

Ron: Do you ask your experts for previously issued reports either to get a sense of their style of writing or how they present their exhibits?

John: Sometimes, not always. I certainly read reports from experts that I've used. I read a lot of report from experts that are on the other side to figure out where I can trap them or trick them. This is in keeping with my simple, "Life is too short, keep it simple" sort of thing.

            I try to look not so much at what's happened in the past that's relevant. I'm concerned about this case, what we're doing here to win.

Ron: When you read another expert's report or your expert's previously issued reports, what do you find most compelling in a report? Or what do you hope becomes most compelling?

John: What matters most for me is making sure there are no mistakes or carelessness. There can't be a typo. If I cross-examine that expert and there's a typo, that indicates to me that he's careless. He's careless, ladies and gentlemen of the jury or Your Honor.

Harvey: It's a matter of him setting out facts that can't be disputed. These are the facts that he's been given to deal with. This is his analysis. And you walk away at the end of reading his report and saying, "There is no other way to handle this."

John: There's one other thing that we haven't talked about that I look at all the time. Assumptions. Because experts don't know the facts, they're told the facts. I want to know what this guy or lady was told. Sometimes the way to discredit the expert is to discredit the assumptions because the assumptions assume things that aren't fact.

Harvey: But the assumptions are in his report.

John: Yes, they're in his report. You ask a lot of questions about the assumptions. And the thought that you're offloading to the jury and judge is if you find that one assumption was invalid, the whole report goes down the toilet. If it's a material assumption.

Harvey: But you're not impugning the expert in that case, you're impugning the person who gave him that assumption to work on.

John: You are a seasoned, wonderful, experienced lawyer who knows that to be the case; that's not supposed to happen. Put yourself in the shoes of a juror who's listening to this and I guarantee you that while you're impugning the integrity indirectly of the expert by challenging the assumptions, that juror is hearing what you want him or her to hear which is "This is a bad guy." And it will take the lead back.

There are a lot of different things that you can do in cross-examining an expert to challenge that expert's bona fide opinion even when the report is pretty good. Your job is not to say, "You know what, this is the best report I've ever seen. I can't do anything to it. I want to sit down." That's not your job. You have to create a mess.

Harvey: You have to find or create a chink in the armor.

Ron: When you're preparing your experts for their testimony, either deposition or cross, how do you prepare them?

John: The way I prepare them and it's the same with the fact witnesses that I prepare. I am absolutely crushing my witnesses on cross-examination in preparation so they will be prepared for the absolute worst and it's probably not going to be nearly that bad.

When you're preparing your expert's direct examination, you're going to go through things. You should try to make it clean so that you're not bleeding and he's doing what he has to do, you're doing what you have to do. You're communicating in a way that's reasonable and not putting people to sleep. That's important. And then the cross is what I said before.

Harvey: A well prepared lawyer will see what the other side is saying and then deal with it effectively. An expert who's going to represent my client is going to thoroughly comprehend what the other side is going to say in opposition and he's going to know why that opposition is full of flaws, and be able to explain simply why it must be rejected.

You have to see it from both sides in order to do the best cross examination. You cross-examine your expert before you have him testify to see how he's going to answer the question, to formulate the best answer to that question. Some questions can be very difficult to explain away. We have to do the best we can depending upon what the issue is. He's got to be prepared to do the best he can. This is my client's life. And we've got to win. That's what litigators live for.

There's a big difference between a litigator and a corporate lawyer. In corporate law, both sides want to do the deal. It's not about my beating you; we both want it. At the end of the day, we want to do a deal. It's the opposite in litigation. I want to win and you want to win. Two people can't win so someone has to lose.

John: The only thing I would add is that I have learned that a good litigator or trial lawyer – there's a very big difference between those two – is developing strategy in the litigation or even at trial to reach a business solution for the client. We're at trial to win. We're not there to lose or draw. The goal is always to find a business solution because the litigation just for litigation's sake is seldom efficient for the client. I'm always thinking about how I can position this from the minute the case starts or even before that so that we get a resolution that we're looking for.

Harvey: Because we want the client to be happy, we try to come up with the best solution for the client at the cheapest price possible. Litigation is just another form of negotiation.

John: One of the biggest challenges we face is to have the client on board that we need the expert. That's why I said the expert has to be part of the team, he helps in simplifying and not by jumping up and down with joy when he sees one little thing in a thousand-page document.

In order to manage the client's expectation and make sure the client doesn't sabotage his own best interest, everything has to be level and calm. I've dragged many clients kicking and screaming to do a settlement only to have them six months later stating, "Thank you so much. That was the greatest thing you could have done. I was not in my right mind. I was still emotional about it. It was the smartest thing I've ever done. And wouldn't have done it if you didn't make me do it."

We need our experts to be on board with that because their analysis can skew things as they paint the best picture possible and that's not always realistic.

Ron: Tell me a story about when you used an expert, whether it went well or it went poorly on your side or on the other side.

John: More than 20 years ago, I had a trial in front of a wonderful judge, who had been on the Appellate Division in Westchester County. It was a big family squabble business divorce involving real estate and other assets. We had a need for two different types of experts in that trial. One was a forensic accounting expert who was looking for some books and records in valuing certain assets and another was a real estate expert who was an appraiser.

The accounting expert was recommended to me by the then managing partner of Herrick. We had been friends with this guy. He was fantastic. At the outset, he was a little difficult because he wasn't very malleable.

He turned out to be an absolutely stellar expert. When he got to trial, he was utterly credible because he and I had fought the fight along the way and we were 100% in sync by the time he got there.

The other expert also became a friend. He was a real estate appraiser. He was so easy from minute one. Whatever suggestion I made was fine with him. He would change it. He was not as good a witness because he was too malleable and he could be moved.

We ended up doing very well in the case and their testimony was credited. But the difference, for me as a young lawyer at the time, informed me a lot about what I'm looking for. The questions I've answered today are a direct result from that experience. Both were excellent experts with wonderful credibility. They both had experience, but they had different approaches. I learned a lot from that experience.

Harvey: When you're dealing with a business divorce, there are big se-crets you understand in the business. All kinds of secrets – tax issues, restrictive covenant issues, licensure issues. Lawyers who are quick to serve a complaint in a business divorce matter are not necessarily very thoughtful. They want to impress and make a score with the client and show they are tough guys. That approach often does not serve the client well in the area of business divorce.

John: Sometimes the best thing to do is to just sit down and shut up or simply not respond. It can work. I've seen in business divorce cases intelligent, successful people become really dumb because their emotions overcome their intellect and that can be a very dangerous thing.

An expert can play a role in helping the client stay on track. The expert is objective, not subjective.

Harvey: You can have a great expert and out of nowhere your client does you in. You prepared him, he sounded ready in your office and then he gets up on the stand, and he's a disaster. Everything you thought he would be able to do, he, for whatever the reason, caves in. It is not the expert's or your fault. Your own client does you in simply because he decides to go down a path he never told you about before. It's a heartbreak.

John: That's an interesting point. Even the bumbling idiot who had the mistake in his report didn't lose the case because of the bumbling idiot; they lost on liability. The bumbling idiot didn't help because it was clearly just all made up. But it's true.

Harvey: If your client is the type I just described, don't expect a great expert to pull his chestnuts out of the fire.

The expert is a piece that fits in the drama if we look at it as a play.

Ron: Do you find that young associates at the firm understand when to use an expert, how to use an expert? When I went to law school, I only knew about it because my dad was in the business.

John: If we're doing our jobs correctly in training our younger people, then they're learning from me or whoever to always be prepared. They learn to be more prepared than you think you need to be. They learn to be thoughtful and manage everybody's expectations. That would include thinking about when to use experts.

I don't think they know that when they come out of law school. I didn't. A lot of cases don't require expert testimony.

I think we do a pretty good job of including our young associates. And they start to think about this if they get involved in the right cases. If the case calls for expert testimony then they see it and it becomes a part of their world.

Harvey: I can't think of an associate in our firm who would be hiring and dealing with an expert without some supervision from a partner. It's not his call without supervision.

John: On the other hand, the youth are taking over the world, as it should be. And if one of the people that works with me says, "I think I know the right person for this issue," I'll talk to that person to figure out if that's the person who will be the best at getting the points across.

Harvey: New associates would want guidance and help and assistance on how to deal with it.

Ron: I want to open it up in case there's something you wanted to share.

John: I think you did a very good job outlining the issues and you asked good questions. You've got some good material to choose from.

CHAPTER 4

PETER GUTOWSKI

Ron: I'm here with Pete Gutowski. Tell us a little bit about your background and what cases you work on and what you do?

Pete: I'm a partner with the firm of Freehill Hogan & Mahar LLP. We are an international transportation and commodities firm. We deal in all aspects of international transportation from casualties to contractual disputes to purchase and sale agreements and commodity sale agreements. I get involved in most aspects except for personal injury cases.

I graduated from Columbia University in 1978 and Tulane Law School in 1981. I've been with Freehill since then. We handle the types of cases described above, both in arbitration and litigation, primarily in New York although, occasionally, we will travel if a client would like us to handle something outside the New York metropolitan area.

Ron: This book is about how litigators win their financial disputes and it's geared towards when they use financial experts. How do you determine where to seek an expert when you want to use one in one of your cases?

Pete: More often than not, we do it either based upon the stable of people we have used in the past or from a referral. Occasionally, we also use the Web. Sometimes we will look for similar cases and then dig for the experts that were used in those cases so we can avoid reinventing the wheel if possible. But it's through a combination of those tools that we end up finding an expert.

Ron: How often would you say you actually find somebody off the internet?

Pete: More often than not, we have good luck using the internet. It's not the primary means by which we find people. As I said, more often than not, we work from referrals, or use someone else we've used before, or someone who has testified in a similar case that we think would be helpful given the particular facts or nature of the claim at issue. Then we use the internet to try to vet that person a little bit more.

Ron: When you get a referral, is that typically from one of the other partners in your firm or somebody you know from another firm?

Pete: It's a combination. It can be from inside the firm or outside. Sometimes it's just a cold referral. I also may call other lawyers I know and ask them if them if they have had experience with an expert in a particular area. Sometimes I will cold call the counsel in a case that is somewhat similar to ours to ask whether they'd share the experience they had with their expert, if I can't find them through PACER.

Ron: When you're searching for the best expert for the specific case you're working on, do you look for that niche guy, that guy who has testified about, for example, freight/cargo ships that travel in Asia? Or are you looking for a lost profits expert? Or a professional expert witness?

Pete: Sometimes it's hard to find a niche guy. They're just not around. The occasions are unique that you need them. You have to find somebody with a little more general background, but we look for somebody that brings a balance to the presentation.

I generally try to shy away from a pure academic expert. We prefer somebody who has been in a field, has the education and expertise, and has testified a number of times. In that way, you get somebody that's tried and true. But it's often hard to find a specialized niche person especially where you have a specialized case. And in that situation, it is even more challenging to find someone that's testified before in a similar case.

Ron: Are there certain credentials that your expert must have?

Pete: Certainly they need qualifying degrees. You don't want somebody testifying that is unable to support the opinion being offered on the basis of a lack of education. We don't see a lot of attacks on people if they have decent credentials, for the most part. But that really isn't the focus in cross-examinations. So long as you have some decent credentials, we're happy with that. It doesn't add or detract too much from the mix after that.

Ron: Do you prefer a professor, an academic type, a professional expert witness, or a practitioner of traditional accounting?

Pete: A mix of the last two. Not to disparage the academics that we have used in the past but they can be subject to criticism if they have no practical experience.

         This said, there are times where you need an academic, especially if you're in a foreign proceeding and the judge there indicates that he or she wants someone to assist in providing the court with an explanation of a particular point of US law. We've had experiences in China where the court has asked for that type of an expert.

Ron: Sometimes the Judge will direct you to what type of expert you need to use?

Pete: In some foreign cases where U.S. law applies by agreement, the court has asked specifically for input from an academic expert, and often we end up with competing opinions from two qualified people. We have been asked to do this in China and Germany. The more persuasive and supported opinion often carries the day.

Ron: I think that's an important point to make based on your experience. I was going to ask you later in the interview but you brought it up about how reports are written and if they're easy to understand or not or how much editing that you need to do. Tell me how important is it for experts' reports to come to you as clean and easy to understand versus how good they are on the witness stand or how much information and how educated they are?

Pete: It's hard to answer that question because you get different quality reports from each individual you encounter. We use experts for all types of unusual situations such as cases involving fires, collisions, weather, as well as contract disputes involving sophisticated damage calculations. Some experts come into the case and really bring something to the table; others may have good credentials but need to be directed in order to remain focused on the issue.

         When an expert comes to you and gives you a product that is clean, supported, understandable, and makes the points you think are valid, it is of immense help. But you have occasions where experts come and you have to have them teach you a bit or provide direction as to where the goal line is

         It's a mixed bag. And sometimes it's tedious to have to work on structure. We find that the more time you put in at the front end to the project, the more you get in the final product.

Ron: Do you inquire or does it matter how often an expert has been on the defendant side or plaintiff side of a matter?

Pete: Yes, and generally only if it is lopsided. If an expert has testified 95% of the time for one side, even if we're on that side, we will have elevated concerns that the expert may be subject to criticism for being biased.

         We look for a person who is fair, honest and balanced because that's the type of person that can withstand cross-examination. That type of person generally does not take too rigid or too extreme a point, and gains credibility by being able to see both sides of the fence -- but at the same time supporting the position you are advancing.

Ron: What are some of the essential traits and characteristics you can identify in a financial expert that you look for?

Pete: We want someone ethical. If there's anything shady about his/her methodology, that will come out. We want a detail-oriented person because this is the nature of the business. It is important that they know the file, and can convey confidence on cross. The expert cannot appear to lose composure. Analytical skills are key because the questions are going to come at the expert live on cross-examination, and the individual has to be able to understand why they are being asked a particular question as much as what the answer is. The expert needs to be able to look forward from the questions and see where the building blocks of impeachment are being placed around him/her and to be able to deal with that.

Ron: What are some of the core skills that you identified that they need to possess?

Pete: They have to grasp the litigation strategy for sure. They have to know where we want to go. And they need to have the fortitude to tell us if we can't get there or we can only get part of the way. They need to be quick on their feet. If you're prepared, you can be quick on your feet, and that's the key.

We don't use experts to investigate things as much as we use them to analyze the facts. So I would say, going back to the points we talked about earlier, understanding the litigation strategy, being able to stay calm, knowing your field and then knowing the file provides the platform to withstand cross-examination and potentially score points. Those are the big ones. We're interested in strategic thinkers and if the expert can bring that to the table and add to the strategy, that's very helpful.

Ron: When a forensic accountant is ineffective, what can you identify as being the most frequent reasons for that ineffectiveness?

Pete: One reason is that they make something too complicated. Even if it is complicated, their job and our job as lawyers is to take the complicated and make it understandable and straight forward. When the testimony or report is too complex, that works to the other side's advantage.

Another thing ineffective is when an expert overstates the position, or portrays that he/she is right on everything. There are times when an expert needs to appreciate when to concede a weak point even though it may not necessarily serve the case. We had a recent case where the opposing expert in a multi-million dollar case tried to attack every aspect and reduce the damages to zero. It was just not credible and he was determined to be ineffective by the tribunal and his opinions ignored.

This is the risk in being too complex and overstating the position by trying to win every point.

Ron: Do you think if that expert had agreed that there were some damages, maybe $100,000 rather than zero, that it might have been more effective?

Pete: I think that there were legitimate points in the dispute about how to calculate the loss in this particular case. But he professed to be right on every single one and it was not a black and white damages case. It was a combination and his rigidity and the complexity of his report detracted from his presentation.

Ron: At what point in your litigation do you hire or retain an expert?

Pete: Generally, it is well before the pleadings stage but it depends upon the complexity of the case. If the case presents a very straightforward damage assessment, we may not use an expert. If it involves things about which we're not completely familiar and comfortable with, or if we think the client is overreaching, then we'll bring somebody in as early as possible. We do this to get a better handle on what the true exposure or the recovery is and to lower expectations where the client has a distorted view of what is achievable. We tend not to wait too long if it's a big case.

Ron:	Are there drawbacks to bringing in an expert early on the case?

Pete: Except for the expense, I don't think so. It either validates what you think or it can help reshape your thinking so you don't go too far down the road and make a mistake. I don't think there's any real drawback in bringing somebody in early.

Ron: Do your clients ever ask you what the hourly fees are for the expert you want to bring in? Do they request that you bring in somebody that has a lower hourly rate?

Pete: Everybody's cost conscious, without a doubt. Oftentimes if we recommend somebody and they don't have any experience in finding someone like that, they're reluctant to buck the recommendation. There's a certain momentum there, especially if there's an underwriter involved and the underwriter has confidence in us. If the client has confidence in us, more often than not, they'll go with it.

We have had occasions where the experts have been very expensive and there is thus some resistance. It's a mixed bag. More often than not, we don't get a lot of resistance on the cost.

Ron: How do you strategize with your experts?

Pete: On complex financial matters, we look to them for guidance about our preliminary ideas of recoverability or potential defenses. Often, the facts exist when the case comes to us, but on some occasions, we are involved during the progression of the dispute. On strategy, there is generally an introductory period when we get the information to the expert to digest and then make a game plan for what the best strategy would be to put together a product. It's done case by case.

Ron: When you're developing your discovery requests, do you ask your financial experts for help in developing them?

Pete: Yes, we try to always do that. We generally send it to them so as to enhance their understanding of the merits and where the battle lines are drawn. We ask: Have we used the right terms?

Are there topics we've overlooked?" Sometimes before you even start to draft it, we'll talk to them and make sure we're headed in the right direction.

Ron: What have you found to be one or some of the most compelling components in an expert's report?

Pete: It has to be understandable. Most of the people that read it are sophisticated so you draft it for your audience. But even with sophisticated people, if they're not well-versed in the financial world then too many financial buzz words may cause confusion.

This goes back to those core elements we discussed earlier which need to be clear, supportable and to the extent it can, tell a story. It makes it more easily understood. Sometimes you can't tell a story in a financial matter but short, declarative sentences that communicate the building blocks both factually and theoretically that get you to your point are the guts of a good report.

Ron: Do you ask your experts for previous reports they've issued to get a sense of their style, or does that matter because you're going to help shape it anyway?

Pete Yes, particularly if the prior report is on the same specific topic. We try to make sure that we're not in any sort of an inconsistent situation that might come up later when we're waist deep in advancing a particular position. But for the most part, when somebody comes through a referral, and you have had a chance to vet the expert, they will reveal any inconsistent opinions that may be out there lurking.

Ron: When you're preparing your expert for testimony and you're going to do direct, do you sit down and prepare with them? Are you confident that they've been with the case for long enough that they know it? How do you prepare them?

Pete: Even when I'm confident that they can do it, I always sit down and prepare. There are two phases to the preparation. The first is an overview of the whole case. We'll review the whole case, what the facts are, what the documents say to ensure that we're all on the same page. The second is to run through with the expert what I would like to achieve both topic wise and question specific.

I make it a practice never to give a script. I find it to be better for cross-examination to cover topics but not to rehearse specific questions because the expert can become a slave to the script and then, when the opposition take the expert off menu, he's lost.

I generally deal conceptually with what we're going to cover, and then let the questions flow. I prepare an outline for myself, obviously, but I don't necessarily give it to the expert other than through dialogue. He can make notes or whatever will help, but I don't want him/her to feel like we are tied to a specific order or sequence. If the expert is prepared to deal with the topics but not necessarily in any particular sequence, I find that it's a better wat to prepare the presentation.

For cross, it is equally important to try to think outside the box, so to speak. You try to identify the weaknesses in the case, and the documents that may present thorny issues, and then we review them in advance. We try to get a handle on where legitimate responses can be framed to those points.

It is equally helpful to avoid saddling the expert with the obligation to win every point. As I mentioned above, certain things sometimes have to be conceded. It's not the expert's fault and he/she shouldn't feel the need to climb over every mountain if that is unachievable.

Ron: When preparing to depose or cross opposing experts, do you strategize with your own expert?

Pete: Oftentimes, yes. We'll go over the report, where we think the holes are, etc. On this topic, there are two schools of thought. Some people beat up the expert in a deposition and walk away feeling that they've done a great job. By the time trial rolls around, there can often be a marked difference in the witness because he/she knows what you've already got. There is a balance between a full on attack at a deposition and saving something for the court or arbitration.

Or you can ask a series of pro-forma questions at the deposition, go through background, report supports, preparation, etc., but save the tough questions for cross. This technique can be risky because if there are things the expert knows can be thrown back at you on cross, and having not asked in the deposition, you can flounder.

In the balance, sometimes there is a benefit in not exposing your hand at a deposition. And that's something I will talk about with the expert because you'll need his input to see if he thinks your instincts are correct about where the weak points are. What I've done a couple of times, which has been effective, was to give the impression of giving up with the opposition expert at the deposition, and leaving the expert with the feeling that he/she was untouched. That often engenders less preparation by the expert for trial.

Like I said, this can be risky because you are asking questions about which you do not have prior answers. But when it works, and if you have the support of your expert, it can be very effective because the opponent's expert is not prepared.

Ron: Will you share with our readers a story about when you have used an expert and how you used him or her? You know what prompted the need to find one?

Pete: When you get into sophisticated calculations of damages, it is very useful to have an expert at your side.

We had one interesting case where the other side's expert's report was very complex. Our expert's report was very straight-forward and down to earth. There were no depositions because it was arbitration. Each expert was permitted a rebuttal report. The rebuttal report by their side was equally opaque and so we opted not to cross examine him at the arbitration because we felt we had a better opportunity to discredit his opinions in a brief where the expert would have no chance of rebuttal testimony. It worked.

Ron: That's a great story. And then to wrap it up, I have one more question. Then, if there's anything else you would like to add, please feel free to do so. Does your firm's young associates have knowledge regarding financial experts? Or do they need to be educated? I know that they're not retaining them, but do they have a sense of when one should be brought in on a case?

Pete: I would say that it depends upon the associate's background. If they have some financial background, they're going to be miles ahead of the person who has none. I think it's just a function of who we have.

Ron: Great. Is there anything else you would like to add?

Pete: Every case is a different, but in matters involving sophisticated damage calculations or complex loss of profit arguments, we have had great success with financial experts who through their education, experience, and training can truly enhance the prospects for success.

Ron: Alright, I appreciate it. That was a great interview, Pete.

Pete: It was my pleasure and I'm happy to participate.

CHAPTER 5

MARTIN KARLINSKY

Ron: I'm going to ask you to introduce yourself - your name, practice, what type of law you practice.

Marty: Sure. Martin Karlinsky or Marty as people usually call me. I practice commercial litigation; most of my work comes from the financial services industry. I have done virtually everything there is to do in litigation from patent litigation to securities litigation. The bulk of my practice today is contract- and commercial based – breach of contract, breach of employment agreement, business tort. I've been practicing for over to 42 years now.

Ron: Have you always been in New York?

Marty: I went to law school at the University of San Francisco. I clerked as an extern clerk for a federal judge out there but never worked in a California firm. I'm admitted in California and occasionally still practice there, usually in federal courts.

I came back to New York after law school and started practicing with a major firm called Shea & Gould which was a hard-hitting business litigation firm back in the 70's, 80's and early 90's. Great firm, great place to start.

Ron: Nice. I'm surprised you went out to California though.

Marty: I was out in California backpacking and climbing mountains, and wanted to stay so it wasn't so surprising.

Ron: How do you determine where you find your experts?

Marty: A couple of different ways. I have experts I've used in all the types of cases that I practice in. I'll go back to the same experts frequently, especially if it's in the damages or economic loss area. There are people that I've used pretty consistently over the years, and I'll use them again when I have the need of a more specialized expert. I can think of a recent insurance coverage case where I decided to use an expert on custom and practice in the insurance industry. That is how most insurers would conduct themselves. The particular case we're talking about is a Directors and Officers Liability Policy.

In that case, to locate my expert, I used another long-standing expert who has served in the role of identifying witnesses for me over the years. I've asked them on many occasions to locate several experts for me to interview and to consider.

I know they have multiple sources, frequently looking at publications, industry reputation, etc. They come up with interesting choices for me; frequently from academia. I find that they are better researchers in the business arena than lawyers typically are. They are MBAs. They are a firm of economic consultants, economists, and damage consultants. I frequently use them as consultants, not as testifying experts. And I will charge them with finding a testifying expert.

Ron: So that you'll retain them?

Marty: Yes, I retain this particular firm in many cases. They're a firm I've used for almost 30 years. I have relationships with them that are disqualifying in terms of them testifying. I'm too close to them and we do too much work together. But it's a firm that I frequently use to help me review other expert's work, to help me locate other experts, and frequently to do background consulting expert work for me which will not involve testifying.

Sometimes, to do almost all of the background consulting work and choose the testifying expert helps to inform the testifying expert. Of course, he or she must accept the underlying work as valid.

Ron: Interesting. And do they begin to write the report?

Marty: Usually not. They usually produce work product like economic analysis. But the report itself, we would typically give to the testifying expert but with their assistance. Sometimes with my assistance; it depends. We do have a very clear ethical obligation both to encourage and to permit the testifying expert to produce a report that is truly his or her work product.

That's an ethical line that I try not to get too close to it. It will have to be the expert's report. That's what the Federal Rules of Civil Procedure contemplate, and I keep it that way.

Ron: What are the areas of specialty you believe are appropriate for a financial expert?

Marty: Of course, the principal area is economic loss or damages. Frequently questions of valuation. I would add anything in the financial services industry requires an expert. It typically requires someone to translate into lay terms what's happening within a private equity firm, hedge fund, trading desk.

Sometimes this can get extremely complicated. I recall a case a few years back involving securities lending, an area that I thought was relatively straightforward. However, the more I became involved in the case, the less straightforward it became. And the more involved it became and proving our case became more involved, we ended up with a testifying expert from the Wharton School who was one of the leading experts in this area of the securities world.

Virtually any financial dispute, business dispute, that arises in the financial services industry - banking and securities, hedge funds, trading, securities lending - is a case which needs an expert. The other area where I have frequently sought out experts is trust and estates litigation. Usually, it's damages consulting; frequently it's forensic work.

We're in New York City and one of the great sources of wealth in this city is real estate. The real estate families in the city become involved in trust and estates litigation a lot. I've represented many New York trustees, beneficiaries, land owners in disputes either arising out of a trust or an estate or in connection with the administration of an estate and trust. In those areas, someone who knows New York real estate, and is a real estate expert, is very useful.

Not just forensics but also real estate. I'm thinking about a particular expert who not only is an accountant and, therefore, suitable to do the accounting work, but he also happens to be an expert in New York real estate and has served as a trustee of large trusts. In that arena, I've also found it very useful in terms of applying standards and whether standards have been met or breached in the real estate industry in New York.

I would add accounting malpractice claims. But you noted that, I think, that in general business disputes, experts are frequently useful. The answer to that question, that is whether to retain an expert in a general business dispute, is two-fold.

One, I look for whether I'm going to need someone to translate to the trier of fact – judge, jury, arbitration panel. If I do, I'm more inclined to seek an expert. That is if the matter involves some specialized subject then it's almost ipso facto. Second, if I need someone to help me understand. There, I'm looking for an expert that may not be a testifying expert but rather a consulting expert.

In the general business dispute world and commercial litigation, I'm always thinking about experts. The rules now in the federal courts require us to. They require the identification of experts pretty early in the process of litigation; sometimes too early I think.

We're basically required by the rules to assess that question, and do, all the time. Sometimes I'll just have a preliminary chat with one of the people I use frequently to say, "Is there something you think you could add to this case?" And often that person will say, "Yes, and here's what it is." Sometimes that person may say, "Not really. That's just not necessary here." I trust my experts to give me their honest evaluation and they seem to do so.

Ron: You did say that sometimes you think you're required to bring an expert on too early?

Can you give me an example?

Marty: The initial disclosures under the federal rules require the identi-fication of experts pretty early in a case before actual discovery commences, but just after the pleading phase is done. I have found that sometimes that is simply too early. Then we tend to reserve our rights in connection with initial disclosures specifically be-cause of that.

I don't know that at a particular other juncture in a case that's governed by the federal rules or a state code analogue would sug-gest another really good time for it. It used to be that experts were identified at the close of actual discovery. I think maybe that's too late. It's a hard choice. I have also found frequently that we have not gotten to the point where we know enough about the case to know that we're going to want an expert at that initial disclosure stage.

Ron: Are there certain credentials you require your experts to have?

Marty: Obviously, I'm going to look for a credentialed expert. Essentially because of the gatekeeper role that the courts play in the expert area, I am looking for someone clearly credentialed, if not only by education, then by training and experience too. He or she has the right credentials to give the testimony required in that area.

That's the test that we've all known for years as well as the more recent refinements like Daubert.

I look for someone who's a teacher. I've always thought of experts as teachers; particularly good ones. I've always thought of them as people who can teach a jury of lay people or a judge or an arbitration panel about his or her subject matter in a way that is interesting and compelling. I'll give you an anecdote if you'd like.

I'm thinking of a particular forensic document examiner whose name I'm not going to mention. He was quite well-known in New York circles and in litigation circles. I remember once putting him on the stand; he's an ideal professor or teacher. Among other things, he loves to teach about what he does. It's not just the opinions he's giving, it's the process of forensic document examination - the science and the art of it.

He comes from a family of forensic document examiners. Both his mother and father were forensic document examiners. They were Jews who lived, I believe, in Vienna before the Holocaust and lost most of their family in the Holocaust. For years, using their specialty knowledge of forensic document examination, they were involved in the search for Nazis. The parents are now deceased. When I put the expert on the witness stand, I ask him to tell the jury his story - why he became what he became. He goes into this wonderful story about his parents, usually with tears in his eyes.

It always has quite an effect on the jury. And on me sometimes too.

Ron: That's a great story. It gets to his sincerity.

That leads into my next question as you said you preferred a teacher. Does the teacher necessarily need to be in academia or just somebody who can teach?

Marty: Somebody who has a natural ability to teach. I'm looking for the best witness, and I think the best witnesses are teachers. They're people who explain and recreate a reality that occurred outside of the courtroom inside the courtroom for the trial. Earlier in my career, I'd liken it to a director in a play or a film putting together an event that happened or a series of events as we might call them transactions or occurrences in litigation and bring them to life for a trier of fact. And teachers do that as do storytellers.

Storytelling is a bit of the aspect of what I'm looking for in an expert. But I prefer to think of it as someone who can teach. I want them to teach ultimately the truth of what they have concluded in the case. And in that manner, assist the trier. One hopes that results in an outcome that's in my client's favor, because that's the end game.

Ron: That answers, to some effect, my next question. What are the core skills to identify in a forensic accountant? What do they need to possess?

Marty: For purposes of testimony, it is teaching and storytelling ability. I always look for experts who have been through examination before; who've testified before; who have the ability to withstand cross examination in the sense that they are neutral and don't feel that a cross examiner is attacking them even though a cross examiner may be doing so. They don't get their backs up or argue with cross examiners.

I've rarely had difficulty with an expert standing up to the onslaught of cross. Usually, they're terrific at it. But I always have my eye out for how the experts will react in that situation. I look for people who are self-starters, who take the initiative, who are making suggestions to me about my case. I very much enjoy working with experts who go beyond the typical role that an expert fills, but can add something to a case. And frequently, they can. An expert witness is someone who brings expertise to a litigated matter and they have a different viewpoint on cases, on juries, on process than I sometimes do. It's very useful. It's great to hear the other perspective and sometimes it teaches me a lot about my own case and helps me present the case.

So, basic skills, other stuff? Diligence and timeliness go without saying. My experts were always very attentive and diligent and timely. They do their work and fit into the case.

Ron: Either on your side or you've seen it on the other side when a forensic accountant has been ineffective, are there reasons that you can identify?

Marty: Frequently, it's because counsel doesn't level with the expert. There are facts that the forensic accountant is not aware of and should have been. There are areas of concern that haven't been fully explored. It's usually lack of preparation or the terrible mistake of keeping things from an expert. That never should be.

If you're in that position, you're probably better off not having an expert. You're going to lose the jury or judge or panel with that expert if it comes out that the expert should've known certain things that she or he doesn't know.

Ron: You mentioned earlier that you identify your experts according to the rules. When do you actually retain them? When do you like to?

Marty: Sometimes before we bring a case. At least of late, we principally have been plaintiff's lawyers. More plaintiff than defense oriented. Other times of my career, I've done more defense work. My answer to the question, as a general answer is, as early as possible. As I noted before, sometimes the rules require a little bit too early. If I have a case where I know I'm going to need an expert, I'm apt to hire the expert early. In large part, because experts add something. I've frequently had experts consulting with me on the structure of a case, on crafting a case, on crafting the complaint in the case. I find that they perform a role at that stage. And they'll very frequently suggest to me areas of either factual or legal inquiry that can be useful before the cases commenced at the onset of the case.

As a general rule, it's something I'm thinking about pretty early on. If it's a case in which I'm going to retain an expert, I frequently will do it early.

Ron: Any drawbacks to bringing the expert on early?

Marty: The tendency to share perhaps a little too much with the expert sometimes. We're no longer worried about core work product than with the revised federal rules. I still think you must worry about it a little bit and protect it.

There's danger with the testifying expert not being too knowledgeable about your case, but on the inside of the case. Your expert is an independent witness. While she or he may be rooting for you in some way or perhaps for your client, I want them to maintain a professional distance. And I want that distance to feel like it's a real distance in the courtroom or the arbitration conference room or whenever a trier is assessing their testimony.

I had this firm of economic consultants who I frequently use on the inside. We were way too close for me to put them on the witness stand. I just don't feel that I can do that. They share too many ideas about the development of cases with me. It would be inappropriate to hire them as an independent expert because they're truly not anymore.

Ron: Would they be seen as a hired mouthpiece?

Marty: Yes, pretty much so.

Ron: You mentioned that you like to bring your experts on and sometimes they help you strategize with your case. How do you work with them to do that?

Marty: I share pleadings with them, brainstorm with them, have breakfast with them and just talk about not only the case but life in general. My life and my work are sort of one piece. Working with my experts means to some extent having business socializing with them. I learn things about them, they learn things about me;

all of that works to assist the case. It helps to build the bond with the expert.

Subject to the question of the independence of the expert, I like a finder to understand that I as the examining attorney have a certain bond with an expert witness. I like it to seem, and to be, a bond of respect – mutual respect. I like the conversation in the courtroom with the expert to be on a high level. When I said before that I look at an expert as a teacher. I think a trial lawyer is a teacher too. It's that dialogue between those two commentators - teachers, professors - in the courtroom that, at its best, is the real way to present reality play in the courtroom.

Ron: Are there any risks/challenges when you sit down with them?

Marty: We come back to not wanting to share everything in your arsenal with your expert. There are strategies and tactics you mean to keep to yourself. There are issues in the case that the expert needn't be involved in, shouldn't be involved in. You don't want the expert to be distracted from her main goal in the case.

I keep using the gender mutual terms her and him. And as I'm thinking of it, I realize that it's very rare that I see a female expert witness.

I never thought about it before. It's rare, especially in forensic accounting. Typically, it's the elder on the team, and usually it's the man who's testifying. I don't know much about the gender composition of the accounting industry. But I don't think I've ever had an occasion to call a woman expert witness.

I'm going to have to make an effort to correct it.

It seems to me that a testifying expert who's female is going to bring a different perspective to matters as differences in gender tend to do.

Ron: Now I want to dive a little bit into your discovery.

When you do discovery and how you develop your discovery requests.

Marty: If it's a technical matter, I'll frequently just ask an expert for the expert's own thoughts. I'll ask the expert to draft not the request, but the list of specific items the expert would like to see. I rarely, if ever, take such a list and incorporate it verbatim into a document request. I'm always "expertising" things that an expert gives me. Frequently, I'll turn to the expert and ask that. It's almost an essential. It's certainly among the roles that your expert is going to play for you.

Ron: Do you ever ask your experts how many times they've testified on behalf of the plaintiff side or the defendant side?

Marty: I do and I tend to like experts who have testified on both sides. I think that the trier of fact cares about those kinds of things. I've had experts who've been purely defense or purely plaintiff side. It's fair game on cross examination, so I try to defuse it in advance. I like my experts to play both sides of the street.

Ron: In your experience, the trier of fact is concerned about that?

Marty: I think so.

I've encountered juries in post-verdict discussion who have remarked on it. So, I have to think that it matters to people. Especially if it's not just plaintiff's side/defense side, but industry versus consumer or some analogous kind of situation. I would consider it something to be very aware of, concerned about and, if possible, to be avoided. Take your financial services industry person, that person who testifies always for the major banks. You can paint that person into a couple of tough places if you're a cross examiner. So better for me if I'm on the plaintiff side in such a case. But not a very good job of choosing, if I'm the lawyer choosing the expert.

Ron: Pertaining to damage reports, do you ask for experts' previous reports to review?

Marty: Rarely.

              In my career, I've seen a few other reports from my experts.
              Sometimes just in hiring an expert, I've seen a few. As work
              product, they are typically not very happy about sharing them
              and there are usually reasons for that. There are confidentiality
              orders in cases and you don't want to have to go through deter-
              mining whether or not you're in compliance. It's a lot easier just to
              skip the step. There have been cases where I have examined other
              reports the expert has done.

Ron: What do you find is most compelling in damage reports?

Marty: A rigorous mathematical analysis that is clear and understandable
              is what I'm looking for. I'm looking also for a damages person who
              understands. I can think of any number of cases using economists
              or CPAs to testify as to matters such as lost wages or future in-
              come, valuation questions like the value of a real property, where
              the damages analysis is something that I'm striving to make as
              clear as I can for the trier of fact. I want my expert to be doing the
              same. And I want my expert, at the same time, to understand the
              legal underpinning of the damages theory.

Ron: When you're getting your experts ready for either a deposition or
              a direct or cross, how do you prepare them for it? Do you spend a
              lot of time with them?

Marty: I used to spend more time. I've tended to spend a little bit less time
              in recent years but I'm thinking of returning to my prior practice.
              An expert can use the refreshment, if you will, of being thoroughly
              prepared as a testifying witness whether in deposition or trial. I
              think that people, even experts, tend to forget some of the basic
              rules; and it's useful to go over. It puts my mind at ease. We owe it
              to our client to do that as we prepare any witness. I'm not overly
              concerned with some of the technicalities because I don't have to
              tell an expert that his deposition is going to be transcribed by a
              court reporter. The expert knows that, but a lay witness may not.

But I do want to refresh them as to the rules. I want to refresh them as to how I conduct myself in a deposition or a trial for that matter. What my theory of depositions is and how I expect the witness to conduct him/herself. I'm a stickler for all that. I'm thinking of returning to more extensive preparation. It puts more of a burden on us as counsel, but that's fine and it helps the expert.

Ron: Do you like your expert to sit in when you depose your adversary's expert?

Marty: I do. It gives my expert confidence in my abilities because that's an important part of the relationship. I have frequently found that an expert sitting in a deposition can be very useful; on balance, more useful than interruptive. On balance the questions or areas of inquiry experts have suggested to me in the course of depositions or before depositions. They've been very, very helpful.

I have even had a consulting expert work up their ideas about the examination which is a step beyond. I have used an economic consulting firm to work up outlines of the deposition examination, not trial. By the time we get to trial, I'm preparing it myself and don't need them. They are useful to prepare for the deposition and to have them sitting in the deposition as well.

We can stream the video and the text in the deposition and someone can be watching two cities away or across the country or across the world and simply email or text in their thoughts as we're sitting there. I find that's a distraction if I am examining. But I will always have my second or a consulting expert receiving that information and data and processing it so that I can use it as I'm sitting there. It works extremely well.

Ron: I'm glad you raised that point about how technology has changed and how we use it.

Will you tell me a little bit more how you see technology has changed the way you use experts?

Marty: Technology has transformed the litigation space and the practice of litigation, and interestingly the principal effect has been to make the process more expensive not less. Depositions in particular are much more expensive these days even though time limited in most federal courts. They are pressured because of the time limitations. Their cost is quite significant when you add the cost of videographers, streaming real-time reporting, and the stenographer. Just the cost of a deposition is upwards of $3,000 to $4,000 a day. And we're not talking about legal fees, but costs. Nor are we talking about the preparation for the deposition, or the processing of the deposition post-completion for use at trial, for use in preparing for trial. Just the actual outside cost.

The cost of it puts us in a position where we have to think very hard about what we want to get from the deposition. We must plan so that we don't waste our time. In the old days, depositions were opportunities for missing the boat; wasted opportunities for counsel. You still see that today especially with younger lawyers who don't seem to know what the deposition is for. They clearly haven't been taught what the deposition is for.

Technology makes us focus on it. For example, the almost uniform videotaping of the depositions. I can't think of a deposition I've taken without videotaping it in the last seven or eight years. If I didn't, it was of an insignificant witness, perhaps, an unknown party where I was just looking to learn something.

That means we have to be more prepared. We have to be closer in terms of style and substance to the way we examine witnesses in courtrooms because that videotape can be used in a courtroom and is likely to be scrutinized in a manner different than a cold transcript. When we prepare our witnesses, we must do a different level of job because witnesses on videotape are very different than witnesses who are simply dictating for the purpose of creating a court record. I can tell you some horror stories about unprepared witnesses on video who have lost cases.

Ron: Will you share one of those stories?

Marty: Oh sure. I'm thinking about a case about 15 years ago where not an expert witness, but a fact witness, was the direct supervisor of a plaintiff suing under the American With Disabilities Act. This plaintiff was an executive who had an ear injury while flying and became deaf. The entire defense that the defendants put forward was she was terminated from the company for poor performance; not because she had been injured and required an accommodation to do her work. The deposition of her direct supervisor unraveled because he hadn't been prepared and he said something really, really stupid.

That stupid statement came back to haunt the defendants so badly that it was in front of the jury on my opening statement. People have said that I won the case on that deposition. It was an unplanned deposition moment. It was a witness who said something stupid that the examiner, me, heard and understood and appreciated the significance of how stupid it was and followed it. You have to listen to the answers you get from the witness.

Ron: And what ended up happening in that case?

Marty: We won before a jury and got a very significant verdict.

In this case I used three different experts: a psychiatric expert on emotional distress and pain and suffering; a forensic document examiner on personnel records that were suspicious; and an economics expert testifying to economic damages, overall, back pay, and future damages.

Ron: Will you share another story about when you used an economic expert and the result?

Marty: The best use of experts I've ever encountered in my career has been in difficult securities cases that involve securities trading where it's very hard to understand what was happening and where lay people would have no idea. A trader might have an intrinsic grasp with it or a securities industry professional might understand it without the need of expert interpolation, but not your typical trier of fact

But in my case, an arbitration case in which I represented the defense, it required the elaborate charting of how a trade unfolded. What parties were involved in it, how it was executed and the timing of it. Only by expert dissection and depiction of the events in charts and diagrams was I able to convey to the trier of fact what actually happened.

I recall that the light went on while I was examining my forensic expert, who happened to be an accountant. He was an expert in the securities industry as well. And the light suddenly went on over the panel's heads, when that expert testified as to what had occurred. It wasn't the story that the claimant had wanted them to accept. Our clients were exonerated.

I love the use of a particular forensic document examiner, the gentleman I described before. I've used him a couple of times in litigation and that "aha" moment when he testified to when he believed a signature was placed on a document was very impactful – it led to many light bulbs going on. Other experts have also been impactful, in the usual damages case. I don't think that the light bulb goes on so much as the trier listens to damages testimony from the expert and it gives them something to hang their hats on. So they have a structure as well as evidence to fall back on that they can talk about in the jury room when they're in deliberations.

Ron: I just have a one final question.

And then if there's anything else you'd like to add, please. The young associates, do they seem prepared? Coming out of law school, do they know how to use an economic expert?

Marty: Uniformly unprepared. My law school, the University of San Francisco's School of Law, does not come in the Top 100 of the ranking across the country. Forty years ago we had a Trial Advocacy course which to this day may be more advanced than virtually any course in the nation. We partnered with doctors and residents at UC San Francisco Medical School using them as our expert witnesses both plaintiff's side and defense side.

We tried a mock medical malpractice case. My first expert witness ever was a rheumatologist who testified on two diseases, temporal arteritis and polymyalgia rheumatica. I still remember this because I went to the medical library and became an overnight expert. I read everything there was in the library about these diseases. That was a unique and invaluable experience at a very early age, understanding what an expert does for you and how you work with an expert.

It was invaluable for them, also to work with lawyers and see what it would be like either to be involved in a malpractice case as some physicians are at one time or another.

This was a very unique opportunity. I've taught at the National Institute for Trial Advocacy (NITA) for about 20 years and have taught the use of experts. We've done it in NITA courses usually with forensic accountants. That's been very helpful, to graduate lawyers in their first practicing years.

I do not think our law schools do a good job, by and large, at preparing students to be litigators and trial lawyers. I'm almost resigned to believing that the law schools can't do a good job at it, but I can't believe that's really the case. I work with my own law school to do something about it.

In this office, there must be 30 books about expert witnesses. One of the things I did very early in my career was to read everything I could lay my hands on. If it was an expert witness, I wanted to know everything that was written about expert witnesses. You can't learn to be a trial lawyer from books, but you can learn what it means to be a trial lawyer.

You can learn what it means to work with experts, how to prepare experts and how you use an expert even to the point of pattern examinations for experts. Even today, as long as I've practiced, if I have an expert who's somewhat unique in a field that I haven't used an expert in, I will go back to one of standard bibles of trial advocacy, the Mauet books on trial technique. Mauet has model examinations of different types of experts. I have found those model examinations of qualifying different experts to be absolutely letter perfect models for any kind of expert across the board. I urge my associates and those I teach to do the same. Go to the books and find out what the masters have said in the past.

I'm not happy about what I see out of law school especially when it comes to experts. That's an area little taught and there could be a lot more to learn about it. As the world, our financial systems become more complex; the need for experts is only going to grow. There is a need in law schools to teach more about it, I don't know why they haven't grasped that yet.

Ron: Anything else you want to add?

Marty: No, I'm done.

Ron: That's great.

Marty: This could be an interesting book.

CHAPTER 6

GERALD KROVATIN

Ron: Please tell us a little bit about you, what you do, where you practice, what type of law you practice.

Gerry: I practice with my partner, Henry Klingeman. The firm is Krovatin Klingeman; we've been together since 2007.

Henry is a former Federal Prosecutor, former Assistant US Attorney and I do a lot of federal work both criminal and civil. I knew Henry from cases and his reputation in the office so it was terrific for us to form our partnership. I went to Rutgers Law School here in Newark, New Jersey.

When I graduated, I went to Lowenstein Sandler where I had been a summer associate. I was at Lowenstein Sandler for 18 years, 13 as a partner. I had a great run there; worked with a really great bunch of people. I left Lowenstein in 1995 and went into partnership with my friend, Jack Arseneault in Chatham (New Jersey) for 4 years. That was Arseneault and Krovatin.

Jack and I split up in 2000 and I opened Krovatin and Associates here in Newark. Then it was Krovatin and Associates until 2007 when Henry and I formed Krovatin Klingeman LLC.

My practice has always been pretty much the same mix of white collar criminal defense and civil litigation. I feel blessed that it's been a diverse practice so that every case is a little different. We don't have a cookie-cutter practice where we're always doing the same slip and fall or the same motor vehicle accident or the same personal injury case. The criminal cases have a lot in common. I have the best of both worlds in the sense that I have both a great criminal defense practice and good civil practice as well.

Ron: As I said, this book is about how litigators win their cases, their financial disputes, and it's geared to educate more of the younger associates.

How do you determine where you seek your experts?

Gerry: It's basically the same people I've used for years. What we do in terms of both the criminal and the civil practice is define the need and then identify the expert who you've worked with in the past and who you have confidence in. In terms of locating those people, that's more of a word of mouth and recommendations from other lawyers primarily.

Ron: Do you interview an expert if you haven't used them before?

Gerry: Oh yes, I always would. You have to be comfortable with an expert. First of all, you have to know what their view of the case is. If they don't agree with your position in the case, there's no sense in hiring him. You have to have the right chemistry with an expert too. It's very important because you've always got to be looking at the likelihood of a trial. And you have to be conscious of the fact that you're going to need your expert to draft a good report so that you get to trial. If the trial actually goes through, you have confidence in your expert's ability to testify.

Ron: What are the areas of specialty you believe are appropriate for a financial expert?

Gerry: The ability to take a complex set of facts and reduce it to a story, a version of the facts that's clean and simple and easy to understand. In terms of the substance of it, I look to a financial expert for a measure of damages. The expert needs to analyze the facts and help me formulate the theory of the damages to the case and then be able to think it through and be able to articulate that theory further down the road.

Valuation is also something that you look to for a financial expert. Sometimes you're looking for your expert to define a standard of care that will lead to a theory of liability of the case.

Ron: What are the qualifications you seek for in a financial expert?

Gerry: First and foremost, the ability to articulate a theory cleanly and simply. Then they must be willing to get into the facts, because the person who controls the facts controls the case. There are some experts who are full of opinions but don't want to learn and master the facts and then to be able to present them.

Presentation skills are increasingly important. Experts must have the ability to combine verbal testimony with appropriate demonstratives and graphics. People are easier to persuade if they can both see and hear it at the same time.

Ron: Do you prefer having an academic or a practicing CPA or a professional expert witness?

Gerry: I always want a practicing CPA. However, there are times when you need an academic if the theory of the case is a little esoteric.

I was in a class action case a couple of years ago with one of the big New York firms. They brought in a key academic guy, and it was fascinating to work with him.

Ron: What type of class action?

Gerry: Securities. But, I'd much rather start with a practicing CPA. I prefer somebody who's been in the trenches and can relate to common problems and be able to explain them.

Ron: Do you inquire and does it matter how many times your expert has worked on the plaintiff side or the defense side?

Gerry: It enhances your credibility as an expert to be able to say that you've done both. There's nothing better in a criminal case than to be able to call an expert, an agent or an investigator who's had some law enforcement experience and background.

Ron: Will you identify some essential traits or characteristics that you look for from your experts?

Gerry: Analytical. By that I mean the ability to get from Point A to Point B in terms of the theory of the case either from a liability perspective or a damages perspective. I can't emphasize enough the importance of being able to see through the issues in the case and define a strategy with me. I like somebody that challenges me; someone that is willing to debate some of the theories of the case and tell me where I'm wrong. That's invaluable.

Ron: When you've seen an economic expert be ineffective on your side or the other side, what do you identify as being the cause of that ineffectiveness?

Gerry: I have the perfect example. We were in a criminal case and called our expert. It was a mortgage fraud case. We wanted to attack the government's theory about the number of mortgages that were implicated in the fraud and take them apart one by one or in different groups. Our expert had a terrible time. The first question was posed for him – "how many files are at issue in this case? How many mortgage files are an issue in this case?" He was all over the map; he couldn't even count the number of files.

            Needless to say, that didn't cast him the best light in front of the jury. That's an oversimplification, but where experts get in trouble is when they express an opinion or theory that they can't back up with the facts of the case.

Ron: When do you retain your experts?

Gerry: As soon as possible in the case. It depends on the resources that the client has available to dedicate to the case. It's a tremendous case where the client says, "Damn the torpedoes, full speed ahead. I don't care what it costs. You just go out and do it." I can count on one hand the number of clients that have said that to me in my 30 years in practice.

Understandably so because most clients want a budget. They want to know what it's going to cost, so you've got to marry your needs, your fee needs, with the needs of the costs in the case. Experts are the biggest cost in any case.

Sometimes, it comes down to convincing the client of the need for the expert and justifying what turns out to be a not insignificant bill from your expert. In the criminal case, where you're fighting the case, they get it. It doesn't matter if they get it if they can't cut that check.

Ron: Any drawbacks to bringing an expert in early besides the fees?

Gerry: I don't think so. It helps to be able to work with your expert throughout the case. The experts I've used have been helpful in shaping discovery strategy and raising issues for discovery.

Ron: How else do you strategize with them?

Gerry: We strategize the theory of the case.

I've consulted with experts even before drafting a complaint to articulate a theory that you're confident your expert will be able to support. The more you can be in-sync with your expert on being able to articulate a theory of the case whether it's damages or liability, it is very important.

Ron: With regards to damage reports, when you read one, what do you find most compelling?

Gerry: I think the ability to hit the essential highlights of the case. I read the report as though I have to use it either to support a motion for summary judgment or defend a motion for summary judgment.

I want to be sure that there is a clear expression of the opinion that has the magic language to it that there's either a deviation from the standard of care or there's not a definition of the standard of care. Citations to the facts in the case, that support the record; that supports the conclusion of the expert.

It's not so much the length of the report. Sometimes clients think that if, "I'm spending this much on an expert I expect that report to be the size of a telephone book." And I don't agree with that; I'd rather the report be in sync and to the point, hit the high notes and give me some confidence that I'm going to survive summary judgment or get summary judgment.

Ron: Do you ever ask your experts for previously issued reports?

Gerry: I don't think I've ever done that. I certainly ask, "have you seen this issue before, have you dealt with that kind of thing before, what's been your experience?" I can't recall ever asking an expert for a report in a prior case. I don't see anything wrong with that, and I think most experts would be happy to show you what they've done in the past.

Ron: How do you prepare your experts for their testimony either deposition, direct or cross?

Gerry: I typically meet several times with the expert in advance of his or her testimony. I like to do a mock Q&A with them as though it was a run through of their actual testimony. I try to anticipate the adversary's focus on the soft spots in our case. I make sure the expert has a solid 'play the tapes' answer to any of those difficult issues or questions in the case, so I'm not surprised.

The goal in preparing any witness is to talk about how to answer the questions. Presentation is as important as the substance. The expert has to be comfortable with the toughest questions, so the practice is always harder than the game.

Ron: Do you use your expert to help with formulating your questions when you're going to depose your adversary's expert?

Gerry: Definitely. I do that a lot. I think some are better than others with that.

Ron: Will you share a story of when you used an expert that worked out well or didn't work out so well?

Gerry: Sure. I always love to tell this story.

I was representing Bob Lee, who was the founder of the International Boxing Federation, the IBF. The government thought that if they could convict Bob Lee and his son, they could get Bob to cooperate against Don King, who was their real target. They indicted Bob Lee and his son in a RICO indictment, alleging that he had fixed ratings and had taken bribes to set up fights, particularly championship fights. The amounts of the bribes he had taken were huge, far beyond what he was entitled to in compensation from the IBF.

My expert's testimony at trial wound up concluding that the IBF owed him money; not that he was taking more than he was entitled to. It was brilliant. I remember the judge looking at me and shaking his head about the testimony.

Ron: Was that a bench trial?

Gerry: No.

It was a jury trial. Bob Lee Jr. was acquitted of everything. And Bob Lee Sr. was acquitted of the RICO. We beat the RICO, but he was convicted on some of the more minor counts in the case. Judge Bissell gave him a very decent sentence, like 20 months. The government was looking to get him for 20 years. The effort on their part to get at Don King through this prosecution fizzled completely, and my expert's testimony was a big part of that.

I used this same expert in another case, and we didn't get to the point in testifying at trial. That case was difficult to explain the numbers and he did a terrific job in terms of the damages. The carrier had attempted to settle a number of questionable cases quickly and early to exhaust the coverage limits. Their plan was to do away with the obligation to pay the defense legal fees. Their position was the legal fees were going to be partly for liability indemnification clause. That was a good case too.

Ron: What was the result in that case?

Gerry: We settled that case after almost two weeks of trial. Judge Martini, the trial judge, took us in the chambers just as I finished the fact portion of our case. And he essentially brokered a settlement. The settlement is confidential, but significant. We began the critical settlement discussion by saying to my adversary, Arthur Goldstein, who's a friend as well; I said to Arthur, "Are you crazy? Do you really want this case to go to this jury?" He was very good at bringing us together to settle the case.

Ron: Do you find that young associates are unprepared or lacking in the skills or expertise in knowing when to use a financial expert or how to use one, whom to ask?

Gerry: Not really. I think they are all looking for guidance; the more senior lawyer on the team to identify the need, identify the type of expert. I don't think it's a lack of ability or insight into what's needed as much as it is deferring to the guy or gal who's been there before.

Ron: That's all my questions. If there's anything that you want touch upon that I haven't covered, please feel free.

Gerry: I think your questions go to the heart of this process that we all go through in defining what the need for expert testimony is in the case, and figuring out who's the right person. I can't imagine going to trial without a damages expert in any kind of commercial or civil case, simply because it's such an important piece of the case.

Even if you understand your theory of damages, your measure of damages, and how the parts fit together; it's better in terms of the credibility of your case to have an expert saying, "The following $1.2 million was directly caused by the injury in this case or the failure to perform in this case. And as a result of that, the following consequential damages were incurred that wouldn't have been incurred in the case." It gives a level of confidence in the case that you don't get with the lawyers standing up and saying the same exact thing. I can't see going to trial these days without a financial expert.

Ron: Great. Wonderful. Perfect.

CHAPTER 7

BRYAN MINTZ

Ron: The book is about how litigators win their cases when money is involved.

And winning is either obtaining more money for your clients or having your clients owe less money than they would have had they hired a different lawyer. I'm here with Bryan Mintz. Bryan, if you wouldn't mind, can you tell us a little bit about your practice and when you started, and we'll take it from there.

Bryan: Sure. I started in 1999, I finished law school and then did a clerkship in New Jersey with an Appellate judge. I spent a couple of years doing corporate work mostly mergers, acquisition and IPOs at a firm in New York, Kelley Drye & Warren. I left there and went to a litigation boutique firm doing products liability and medical malpractice defense. After that, I moved to New Jersey and worked at McCarter & English for 6 years doing products liability work and also business litigation. I then became a partner in the litigation department of Paris Ackerman & Schmierer in Roseland, New Jersey for about 4 years. In 2015, I joined Mintz & Geftic as a partner focusing my practice on complex litigation involving contract and business disputes, products liability, wage and hour class actions, medical malpractice, and personal injury.

Ron: So again, the book is how litigators win their cases and how they win when they are using a financial expert – a forensic accountant, or an economic expert. In general, I believe lawyers retain a financial expert when they have a dispute about money. How do you typically find an expert that you're going to use?

Bryan: Well, typically, it's word of mouth. Who other attorneys have used in a similar case. Some of it may be venue driven. We may have an expert we like to use in cases in California and one that we'd rather have in New York. And then there is more local disputes. Let's say a dispute in Middlesex County, NJ. We may feel more comfortable using a local accounting firm or forensic accountant from a Middlesex County accounting office, especially if we think it's going to go to a jury trial.

Ron: Is that because you think the expert will resonate with the jury if they're from the same area?

Bryan: I think so.

I mean, all things being equal. I think if an accountant is from right down the street, has all the same credentials as the other side's expert who happens to be from another state; I think there is some local appeal and that the jury might relate better to somebody who has spent their days in the same town they do.

Ron: I was speaking to a lawyer yesterday who has a trial that's coming up in South Carolina and they have local counsel there who said that, "You cannot bring an expert from New York. It has to be a good ole boy. It has to be. The jury wouldn't listen to anybody that's not a good ole boy."

Bryan: I think that there's something to that. Maybe if it's before a judge, it would be little different but certainly before a jury.

Ron: I agree with that. I think that's unfortunate, but I do agree.

Bryan: It's the same reason that lawyers get local counsel in a lot of cases, right? They can get pro hac'd in. But a lot of times, you want a local lawyer.

Ron: Agreed. They know the system, they know the rules.

When you are looking for an expert, are there certain credentials that you require them to have?

Bryan: A CPA is pretty standard. But they have to have the expertise. I mean if they've been qualified. I would never get an expert who's never been qualified by the court as an expert before.

If we have an expert who's experienced and who's been qualified as an expert in various jurisdictions, I wouldn't have a problem. It doesn't matter how many letters are put past their name.

Ron: Which makes it complicated because everybody says, "Oh, you have to have testified"; have some testifying experience, but you have to start somewhere to get your foot in the door.

Bryan: That's correct. I just mean, for my cases and my clients, that is not going to be their first.

Ron: How do you distinguish if you choose someone who's either a practitioner or a professional expert witness versus somebody who's a professor or an academic?

Bryan: That's a good question. I don't think it matters to me. I wouldn't exclude an expert who happens to also be a professor and I wouldn't exclude a professor that maybe isn't a practitioner.

Ron: Typically, I hear attorneys like to use the academics when it's something more complicated. If there's some macro-economic theory that needs to be explained versus lost profits.

Bryan: I could see that maybe the professors who specialize in one certain area of accounting or economics and have written articles about it may make sense. I just have not had a case where it calls for that.

Ron: Do you ask your expert how many times they've testified for the defendant's or plaintiff's side?

Bryan: I ask about their experience testifying at depositions and trials. I do ask if they're defendant or plaintiff side. It doesn't really matter to me. Typically, I think that most of the accountants I've dealt with have done both sides.

You may be a plaintiff, but you've been counter-claimed against so that you're also defending claims. So in those types of cases, it doesn't really matter. You're kind of both.

Ron: Do you actually interview your potential expert witnesses or do you retain them based on word of mouth or referrals or somebody that you've used in the past?

Bryan: It's both. I mean, we would never retain an expert without interviewing the expert. We wouldn't just send out a retainer agreement. We would definitely interview them and do an analysis to see whether or not we think they're right for this litigation. Then we would make the recommendation to the client who's ultimately the one who's going to have to decide in typical commercial type litigation.

Ron: Are there core skills or characteristics that you look for in an expert?

Bryan: There are. Any case that we've dealt with that requires an economic expert has been a pretty high value type of case. I would love to be able to use a forensic accounting firm like yours in every case, but the client just can't always afford it.

Some of the qualifications that we look for are usually already known. We know, for example, your firm and we know you're detail oriented, analytical, and responsive. There are other things that we look to, for example, likeability which is important. Not just because you're going to be working closely with the expert, but the likability factor before a judge or a jury is important. That's something that we definitely look for when we're looking for an expert; somebody that has all the other characteristics that you need - the analytical-ness, the responsiveness, being detail oriented, ethical, responsive to your needs. But you also need somebody who's likable.

Ron: Yeah, that's a great point.

            I've heard a few times people say they also want the gray-haired, mature looking expert, that that's important. I don't necessarily know how important that is, but I've heard it several times.

Bryan: Maybe it is. I don't know. If somebody looks young but knows what they're doing and is likable and has all the other qualifications, I don't think I would rule them out. That's for sure.

Ron: I agree with that. When you use an expert, a forensic accountant, or an expert witness and they're ineffective; what are the reasons that you see that they weren't effective?

Bryan: Fortunately, we've done a good job of selecting the right expert.

            We've been in a very good situation where we didn't have that. Although I've had one case where we did not select the expert, the client did. And it was a case that we took over from another firm. In that case, I don't want criticize the expert, but I think he was ineffective.

            He was ineffective in one category in that he didn't do a good job of pointing out some of the weaknesses in the case to both the client and to the lawyer. Things that were more accounting based that would have been good to know earlier. I don't know if he was just trying to prove his case and neglect the weaknesses.

            But I think a good trait of an expert is to say, "Well, you know, you have some problems here, you have problems there." Devil's advocate. I think that's always helpful because a lawyer who doesn't have an accounting background isn't going to pick up on some of those. You don't want to wait till the other side's expert report comes out or until the deposition of your own expert to realize "Hey, we got a little bit of problems here". That's what happened in that case where something came up when our accountant was deposed where he had to make some concessions. We spoke to him after saying, "Why didn't you tell us there were a couple of these weaknesses here?" And he said, "Ah, yeah. Well, I thought we had a good case and you know..." I said, "Well, it's not a big deal, but it would have been better if we addressed it before your deposition. There's ways to address it; we could have amended your report and things like that."

Ron: Right, good example of when you wanted something from your expert that they didn't provide and that it proves faulty in the end.

You've mentioned before that you would like to have a forensic accountant on all of your financial disputes but it's cost prohibitive for your client. Does that play into when you do retain an expert? I hear experts say they want to be brought in on the case at the beginning. And I hear attorneys say they don't bring an expert in until it's either required by the rules or as late as possible so they don't start incurring fees. When do you bring in an expert?

Bryan: Ideally, if you have a client who can afford it, you want to bring in an expert as early as possible. If it's a case where you are the plaintiff and you're putting together your proofs to file the complaint; a lot of times the parties or your clients have expectation or hope that "Hey, we'll file this complaint, we'll serve it and then they'll come to us and want to settle." It's usually just wishful thinking.

If I had my way I'd say, "Hey look, let's get the expert involved. Let's cross our T's and dot our I's. Put the complaint together, file the complaint and we already have our expert report." If that's even possible, if you have the documents, sometimes you have to wait to get the documents anyway. But if you can get it early, I think that's the best.

If you're defending a case, again, get the expert in early. The expert could also be very helpful in formulating what documents you will need or what they will need to put together their report and under the correct terminology.

I think earlier is better. But I think everybody's always hopeful that they'll be able to resolve the case without paying a ton of expert fees and legal fees, so they put it off for as long as they can.

Ron: That's what I've heard a lot. The hoping to settle, avoid those fees. But if the client can afford it, why not bring in the expert early; why not hear their rationale, the way that they think in terms of damages and economics? Whereas the lawyers, typically, are thinking strategy about how to get the case to settle, about liability.

Bryan: Yes, you're definitely right. Sometimes having an expert involved early and even putting together a rough kind of report may add to the settlement value of the case. I'll give an example. Although it didn't work out at mediation, we engaged our expert for purposes of mediation to put together a damages model. We didn't have to do it. We could have gone in without it but thought it would have been effective for the mediation. It would have increased the settlement value of the case by having our expert on board even though it wasn't required for a mediation.

Ron: And I have to say that's pretty smart thinking.

I see a great value in having the expert come in early especially for purposes of settling. Then the other side sees the strength of their adversary.

Bryan: Right. Then there's also a possibility that you think your case is great and then your expert comes back to you and says, "You have some problems here". It's better for you to know that early on.

The only downside is that maybe you paid for an expert and the case was going to settle anyway.

Ron: Do you strategize with your experts? Do you bring them in and ask them what they think from their point of view?

Bryan: Yeah, definitely.

Ron: Are there challenges with doing that? Because the experts aren't typically lawyers so they're strategizing in a different way.

Bryan: No, I don't think so. As long as you know it's coming from somebody who for the most part, is looking at the numbers. We work with experts who have been doing this for 30, 40 years and they have experience with not just the numbers but how cases appear before a judge and jury. To not value their input would be foolish.

Ron: And you mentioned before that you like to bring in your expert, if you have the opportunity, to help prepare document request lists, which I think is important. When you read an expert's report, what do you find to be the most compelling points in those reports? Does it tell a clear story? Is it that their damages model makes sense?

Bryan: I think it's everything.

When we're prosecuting a case; I flip to the end. I'm going to go to the end to see what's the bottom-line, what's the number. And then I'll read the report and see if it makes sense as to how that number came about. In other words, I'll check the math. That's a good sign if I understand it. If I had some issues after reading it once and I'm a little confused on certain things, then I may ask the expert to make some changes to make it more readable and perhaps bring it into more layman terms

Ron: You definitely need to understand it. Because if you don't then the jury definitely is not going to.

Bryan: I need to understand it to a point where I can explain it.

Ron: Do you ever ask your experts if they can send you previously issued reports?

Bryan: I haven't, no. Our cases are all different, so I don't know that it would matter what they put in their other reports.

Ron: When you're preparing your expert for their deposition or trial testimony, what do you do to prepare them?

Bryan: I have an outline I go over when we prepare witnesses for depositions and for experts.

And every case is, obviously, a little different. When it's for a deposition, we're not necessarily trying to win the case. I tell them keep your answers short and concise and respond to only the question - all the standard instructions. With the trial, it's a little different because you're trying to educate the jury; so that's a little different type of prep.

But for a deposition, most of the experts we've used have done hundreds, so there's not much they need to do as far as the preparation for how to answer the questions and how to give us time to object or anything like that. It's more just going over the substance of their opinion, any weaknesses that they see in the possible cross examination that they may face. We may do a couple of mock questions and answers and a mock cross examination just to see how they're going to respond and give them a chance to practice their responses.

Ron: Is the preparation different than a fact witness because they don't have that experience, correct?

Bryan: Yeah, that's absolutely correct.

Ron: When you're going to depose the opposing experts, do you like to have your expert there in the room to help?

Bryan: I think, ideally, that would be good.

Ron: Do you have a story of a case that you used an expert and how it worked out for better or worse?

Bryan: I told you of one situation where the expert, after we took over the case and where the expert was cross examined on a point at a deposition and had to concede on it. He conceded that he didn't read something; and then afterward he told us he did actually review it and he should have said that at his deposition. It was an important document that needed to be reviewed in order to be a basis for his opinion. I said, "Well, I thought you read it, but why did you tell him you didn't read it?" And he said, "I just completely forgot."

We had to do a certification from our expert and submitted it which gave them the right to then re-depose the expert and ask him what happened. Then he had to explain that he forgot. He did rely on it. Another firm ended up taking over the case too. So it turned out to not be our case in the end. But I think the expert travelled with the case which didn't turn out very well.

Ron: Do you find that young associates know how to use financial experts when they need one, or do they need to be educated?

Bryan: When I was a young associate in big cases, there was never a situation where a young associate was tasked with the responsibility of finding an expert in the case that required a forensic accounting firm. The associate was told who the expert was by the partner who probably got the name of the expert from somebody he'd used in the past or somebody else who had worked with the firm. So I don't even know if there were any situations where a young associate had to do that.

Ron: Right, That's a good point. They probably get their experience and their training on the job learning from the partner they're working with.

Bryan: Exactly.

CHAPTER 8

SAM ROSENFARB

Ron: I'm here with the well-known forensic accountant, Sam Rosenfarb, who also happens to be my father.

I'm interviewing Sam for a book I'm writing primarily for commercial litigators on how they win their financial disputes along with advice from these winning lawyers on how to use financial experts. This book is primarily going to be used by commercial litigators to hand out to their younger associates for insight on using financial experts and how to win their case.

Sam: So, the book is about how litigators can win their litigations – their commercial litigations – which are all about money. Financial experts and finding financial experts, that part of the story isn't interesting, I think, to litigators.

They just want to win. They have concluded that using appropriate and experienced experts - financial experts - is part of that winning. I don't believe that they believe that picking the right financial expert is part of winning.

Ron: Do you believe that commercial litigators choose a financial expert because they are forced to by the courts or because the other side has an expert?

Sam: They're forced to because the rules forced them to; not because the other side has an expert.

Ron: It's an important distinction.

Sam: Yes, right. That distinction is, absent the requirement for a financial expert, they would retain experts significantly less often because the preponderance of the cases wouldn't have experts.

I don't believe they see a correlation between the experts and winning. Request them to list the top 10 reasons why they win cases. Getting the right expert is not on that list. Suggesting that in either the title of the book or your rationale for writing the book would confuse them.

Ron: That said, let's go off my script somewhat and let me ask you some other questions. First, tell a little bit about your background – how you got involved with forensic accounting and how long you've been doing it.

Sam: I was a "regular" accountant. I prepared tax returns, financial statements, and audited financial statements. I represented small closely held businesses; small meaning revenues of less than $100 million.

Most of my clients, in today's volume, would have revenues or assets in the $10 million range. I was their trusted business advisor. I provided them with advice on income taxes, estate taxes, sales taxes, payroll taxes; all forms of businesses taxes. I provided them with business advice on how to generate greater profitability in their business, greater value for their business and greater wealth for themselves and their families.

I did that from the time I graduated college in 1969 until the late 1970s. In the early 1980s I started to concentrate my work in forensic accounting, which is predominantly financial expert witness work. Expert witness work is testifying about financial damages, for the most part. Since the early 90s, my practice has been exclusively working for litigators. I am retained by litigators to assist them in their representation of clients involved in commercial litigation. Predominantly testifying about the damages resulting from breach of contract or tort cases, as well as accounting malpractice cases.

My practice is 80% financial damages, 20% accounting malpractice. Financial damages in all sorts of business disputes, including lost profits cases, breach of contract cases, IP disputes, legal malpractice cases, and estate and trust matters; business divorces, in general.

Ron: That's been a long time. That's the start of what people started calling "forensic accounting", correct?

Sam: Correct. That's 25-30 years, I've been doing that exclusively. I was one of the early settlers in this area.

Ron: When you're being interviewed to be someone's expert witness or consulting expert, what are the credentials that the attorneys require?

Sam: People use me because I've been referred to them by somebody else or I have a relationship with the litigator and he, or she, knows that I'd be right for the case based on our prior experience. It's unusual for me to be interviewed for a case, but that happens once in a while.

I don't really know what the basis is for the litigator's decision to use me or not. I think, to a great extent, they want industry expertise; that if I have experience within the industry that their case resides, that's a big plus.

Being a CPA is a minimum requirement. They would have no interest in speaking to me other than if I were CPA because financial damages are relegated to either economists or CPAs. And since I'm not an economist, I have to be a CPA.

There is no credential for an economist. Almost anybody can call himself an economist. The only credential which is universally accepted is a CPA credential. In addition to a CPA credential, I'm an accredited business appraiser, which is an added plus for most of the cases. I am also a certified fraud examiner – a CFE. These credentials distinguish me from other "regular" CPAs.

It's these credentials, I believe, that influence litigators.

Ron: What do you believe influences these litigators to look for a practitioner versus an academic - a professor or an economist versus a professional expert witness?

Sam: One of the criticisms of me as an expert witness is that I'm a professional expert; not a practitioner. I don't practice accounting, so when I testify as an expert, my profession is expert witness. However, such criticism ignores my many years of practice as a "regular" CPA practitioner. Also, my many years as an expert witness has provided me with skills and information that most CPA practitioners never develop.

So if the question is what distinguishes me from an academic, I think it depends on the issue. I think academics have a role to play. Academics in technical, narrow subject areas are certainly beneficial.

If the area of inquiry of expert testimony requires an explanation of econometric theory, I think an academic is better than a CPA. But if the area of testimony is limited to or revolves around lost profits, who better than a CPA to describe profits that are lost? It is the CPA profession that accounts for profits and that quantifies profits. There is no other profession that is charged with quantifying profits.

Ron: Does your experience as a practitioner, as a public accountant, play a role in your becoming an expert witness?

Sam: Sure, because I have significant experience representing clients both as a trusted business advisor and as a business consultant that gives me standing and background to testify about business issues.

Ron: Or else you'd be motioned out of there quickly?

Sam: Not necessarily. No.

Ron: No? Explain that to me.

Sam: I can have expertise from a pure academic perspective. I don't need necessarily to have expertise as a practitioner. It depends on the subject matter rather than my experience. The subject matter identifies the requisite skills for testifying.

One of the purposes of the expert witness is to provide information to a trier of fact, a judge, jury, panel of arbitrators, or arbitrator that can't be gleaned, can't be understood, can't be developed by lay witnesses, by fact witnesses.

The area of expertise that's required to be elucidated to the judge - to the trier of fact - is one which requires practice. For instance, if the issue is whether or not an accountant performed in accordance with his peers, whether his performance was negligent; experience as an accountant would be required. How could somebody who's never practiced as an accountant have an opinion on whether or not another accountant's performance was negligent? That would be inconsistent.

But, if the subject matter of the testimony is how much money would have been earned, how much profit would have been generated had there not been this breach? That question may not require any practitioner experience. It requires industry understanding. It requires business understanding, but not necessarily practice understanding.

Ron: What are some core skills that you think a forensic accountant needs to possess to be an effective expert witness, forensic accountant, or financial expert?

Sam: Those are significantly different questions. In order to be a forensic accountant or financial expert you don't necessarily have to be good at being an expert witness.

Ron: That's an important distinction.

Sam: The skills required to be a witness, whether it's a forensic accountant, or a medical expert witness, or an engineering expert witness, or a scientific expert witness, are similar. They're the ability to think quickly on your feet because others will be asking you questions on the stand and an expert witness needs to be able to respond in a facile way.

You need to be able to be persuasive and speak in a compelling manner to be able to convince others of your position and opinions. To be sincere, to be credible, and to be expert - which means to have information about a topic that is not generally held with the population, to have specific information.

It's to present yourself as trustworthy, clear, and communicative; to speak without jargon. Those are very difficult tasks for a lot of experts, for a lot of professionals. Accountants have a tough time speaking without debits, credits and roll-ups and AR and AP and GLs. They speak in jargon.

Ron: Do you see that happening even more when there are specific niche industry experts, like an oil and gas guy who can't explain, that has to talk about the viscosity of the oil and where it comes from and something along those lines?

Sam: The industry experts have a much tougher time.

I want to differentiate. The skills of the testifying experts are similar irrespective of the expertise and the focus of the testimony.

That's true of any expert whether it's an industry testifying expert, financial testifying expert, CPA testifying expert, or scientific testifying expert; the skills I've described for expert testimony are the same.

It's very difficult for most industry experts who are not good at testifying or haven't testified frequently, it's difficult for them to be effective. It's not just industry experts or technical experts, but especially CPAs. It's very difficult for them to testify or communicate without jargon.

Ron: It's probably easier for them to write clearly for somebody that's going to have time to read through a report, I would imagine, than actually tell the story clearly and be compelling to a trier of fact.

Sam: I think it's difficult for them to do both; especially for accountants. Accountants are generally very poor communicators and their writing skills are frequently subpar. They have as much difficulty or even more difficulty communicating and writing than in conversation or in testimony.

Ron: Have you been asked by litigators planning to retain you to provide them with some previously published reports?

Sam: No. But that would be an excellent idea. That would be an excellent way for a litigator to evaluate their experts.

Ron: When you're up against an opposing expert, do you try to find their previously published reports, or the identity of other litigators that have worked with them or against them?

Sam: I do, but almost universally without any success because, for the most part, cases settle. 90% of my cases settled so the reports for those 90% of the cases aren't made public. The 10% of the cases that go to trial, a great deal of them are in arbitration and aren't made public either.

The ones that are in court, the reports themselves rarely make it into evidence and so, they are not made public. It's very difficult to get an expert's report from the public domain.

Ron: Are you often asked how many times you've testified on the defense or the plaintiff side?

Sam: I'm often asked that. Although it's a surprising question given what I do. It's a very interesting question for professional malpractice witnesses, for medical expert witnesses as to which side they testify on. But for damage experts, plaintiff or defense side, is generally the same skill set. Coincidently, I am retained almost equally by the plaintiff and the defendant.

Ron: During a deposition, are you asked how many times you've worked with a certain firm?

Sam: Frequently. The other side wants the connection between me and the litigation firm to be closer than it is because it may impede a perception of independence.

If I work very often with a particular firm, they attempt to paint a picture of me being an employee of that firm, in which case, I wouldn't be independent. Therefore, they hope that my testimony wouldn't be credible.

Ron: But they would try to paint that picture?

Sam: Yes. If I was an employee, my testimony may not be permitted. So they may try to preclude my testimony if my relationship is so close.

I remember many years ago, one of the matrimonial attorneys in New Jersey had an expert that he used in every case and the attorney was that expert's executor of his will.

The claim was that the connections were so close that the expert couldn't be independent because his livelihood depended upon that particular lawyer. That fact was significant enough impediment for the courts to determine that the expert shouldn't testify.

Ron: Was that big news in the industry?

Sam: Very big news.

Ron: When do you see a forensic accountant being most ineffective?

Sam: Do you mean, when is a financial expert witness ineffective? Because most forensic accountants in the world aren't expert witnesses.

           The world of forensic accountants, maybe in United States, perhaps, they number maybe 40,000 CPAs who identify themselves as forensic accountants. Of those 40,000, somewhere around 500 have testified more than 20 times.

Ron: Wow, it's a small group.

Sam: It's a very small group. There may be a thousand who've testified more than 10 times. The other 39,000 never intend to testify.

           The bulk of them are retained by law firms or companies to conduct investigations - internal investigations, financial investigations, and Foreign Corrupt Practices Act investigations. Those investigations lead to factual determinations that aren't intended to result in litigation, so they rarely require anyone to testify. Even in a tax investigation.

           Most of the forensic accountants of the world don't perform services that are likely to result in testimony. The skills that are required for testimony are very different than the skills required to perform investigative services.

Ron: When you are retained as an expert witness or a consulting expert, at what point in the litigation are you typically retained?

Sam: I like to be retained early and often. But, I'm usually retained at the time of the litigation when the identification of an expert witness is required.

           Litigators generally retain expert witnesses because they are required to; not because they believe that experts are conducive to promote a settlement or that experts are able to assist them in settlement discussions or to help in the strategy of the litigation.

I'm usually retained late in the case. Most litigators believe that the case will settle prior to the requirement to identify an expert witness. If settlement can be accomplished without the retention of an expert witness; they believe, I think, wrongfully and completely erroneously, that their clients are well served because they haven't paid any funds to an expert witness.

Ron: Do you see those fees as being the main or only drawback to bringing in an expert early in the case?

Sam: Yes, experts would be brought in early if there were no cost.

The litigators don't want to spend time either interviewing an expert or discussing the case with the expert unless they're required to by the rules. It's the client funds that are the primary impediment.

Ron: Do you see that changing anytime in the future - bringing in the expert early in the pleadings stage, help with the complaint, help them think about the case early on?

Sam: The role of expert witnesses has gotten larger and has inculcated more litigations today than ever. That encroachment on litigation has grown every year. So every year, financial experts have played a greater role in the litigation process than in the year before. I think that trend will continue. I believe the rules will evolve so that a litigator will be guilty of malpractice if he doesn't have a strong understanding of the damages in a case when he settles. I think that a recommendation regarding settlement will require some consulting with an expert.

I think that there will be a case where one lawyer settles a case for his client when he didn't consult an expert in the settlement; and did not take into account a specific significant damage theory that was not espoused or directed to the client. If the client becomes aware of that after the settlement and is precluded from pursuing his adversary, he will instead pursue his lawyer in a malpractice case. Such a case will expand the role of financial experts even further.

In New York State, for instance, there's been a significant change within the last few years. The New York State commercial cases are now required to have reports and depositions when they have financial experts.

Ron: Do you prefer writing a rebuttal report?

Sam: It's much more fun to work for the defendant and get to see the plaintiff's expert's report before my report is due. It's much easier to respond to a report than to exchange reports on the same day or write reports that are due on the same day. I much prefer to write a rebuttal report because it's easier to criticize another's opinion than to come up with initial concepts.

Ron: You tell the judge, "Look at how deficient this is…." How often are you brought in for litigation strategy, deposition strategy, or cross examination of your opposing expert, and how much value do you think they place on that? If they don't place enough, why should they place more?

Sam: I'm rarely engaged to assist in developing litigation strategy. My insights are very well received when I am. I believe every litigator should retain financial experts to assist in litigation strategy because financial experts have significantly different perspectives and concepts than litigation experts about damages and facts that could influence damages which aren't considered by litigators.

I'm frequently asked to assist in developing deposition questions for the expert of my client's adversary. But that generally is a task that the litigator's comfortable with since he's asking me as an expert to provide him or her with insights as to my opposing expert. That's common, so the litigator doesn't place much value on that. It's a task that is easily relegated to me without any bruising of his or her ego.

I am less frequently asked to assist in cross examination. Litigators pride themselves on the ability to cross examine and so they don't seek the advice of an expert on that task.

Ron: The ones that do ask you for your input on cross examination, are they, in your mind, better litigators?

Sam: I think the best litigators ask all of their experts for advice - advice on strategy, the opposing experts, cross examination, and direction of the case. Even the best litigators fail to retain experts to evaluate their own experts. I've never had a litigator retain an expert to assist the litigator in evaluating the weaknesses of my report, in my opinions. The litigators rely on themselves to do that. I think to their peril.

Ron: I'd love for you to tell us a story about how a case was won because of the use of you as a financial expert.

Before you do that, if there's anything else that you'd like to tell me that I haven't asked you; that you think is important.

Sam: Every case I testify in is won because of my good work. Winning means getting money, and without my testimony, the client wouldn't get any money. When the case is lost, it has nothing to do with my work. That's because the litigators didn't do a good job and they lost the case. Of course, most of that is said with tongue in cheek.

The financial expert is responsible for getting money. A good financial expert will be able to assist the litigator in telling his story and weaving the issues in the liability part of the case into his damage testimony.

It doesn't always go well when I testify. Some clients have been convicted of criminal matters. Some clients have lost their claim for money.

I don't recall which defendants I've worked for that lost. I can think of a number of plaintiffs that lost or weren't rewarded any damages. But I can't think of a defendant that lost.

Ron: We spoke earlier about the niche experts that commercial litigators look to because of their specific knowledge of a particular industry, such as real estate or trucking and so forth. We've had these discussions before that one could know about a specific industry by studying that industry; or one could be particularly skilled to testify about lost profits because experience as a CPA, including business acumen. Can you expand on that a little bit?

Sam: As a CPA and a business appraiser, I've developed skills and obtained education and knowledge that is applicable to any industry. So I know how to account for profits in various industries. That expertise is not limited to the retail industry or the manufacturing industry or the distribution industry. It's universal.

The skills that I have developed - the appraisal skills, the accounting skills, the business acumen skills – are applicable to any industry. The concept of a profit-making activity is universal. They may not be applicable to not-for-profit organizations or governmental organizations, but they're applicable to every profit making enterprise.

Having in-depth industry knowledge, from my perspective, hasn't helped me. Even when I've had significant in-depth knowledge of a particular industry and I have a case involving that industry, that significant in-depth knowledge doesn't significantly help me with that case. There is a perception that it does, but it doesn't.

The skills regarding my testimony are business acumen: understanding the facts of the case - the instant case - which is always different from every other case and is typically unrelated to the industry.

The facts of the case have to do with people - who did what, to whom, when, and why. The people involved in the case and their activity is unique to the case, and is not unique to the industry in which the case resides. The activity of the people is the essence of the case which is unrelated to the industry. People are the same whether they work in healthcare, retail, or manufacturing.

Ron: It seems like that reality gets lost on a lot of litigators.

Sam: It definitely gets lost. Understandably so, because litigators don't understand the expertise required to calculate damages. They believe that the damages are influenced by the recognition and understanding of a particular industry or category of business.

        When I testified in the Great Lakes dredging case, having familiarity with the dredging industry or the Maritime industry or Maritime law was completely unnecessary. The expertise, understanding, and skill that was required was to understand the motivation for influencing business activity. And that's the same irrespective of the business.

        I think it was lost on the expert for the defendants, and that's what hurt them. Had the defendant's experts been more worldly in calculating lost profits, instead of being focused predominantly as a Maritime industry expert; the defendant would have been better served.

        I testified in the Cohen and Perelman case where the judge sided with my opinion. He understood where I was going and what I said.

        And that had very little to do with estate and trust expertise or real estate expertise. But that's what the lawyers wanted. They were focused on somebody with real estate expertise and the other side was focused on that as well and I think to their peril.

        In many of these cases, I believe that had I been the expert on the other side, they might have won the case. I think the expert plays a significant role in influencing the trier of fact.

Ron: But that's not a universal belief. Maybe amongst the testifying experts it is, but not amongst those that retain those experts.

Sam: I don't even think it's a universally held belief among testifying experts.

        Litigators believe that they win or lose the case. I believe that winning or losing is the result of getting more or less money. Who has greater influence on more or less money than the financial testifying expert?

Ron: Do you want to tell us a little bit about the facts in the Cohen – Perelman case that you mentioned before?

Sam: It's about a father who owned a business whose son worked in the business. And over the years the father was influenced to transfer interests in the business to his son. The father had a daughter who died prematurely. She was married to Ron Perelman who's reputed to be worth $14 billion. They had a child, Samantha Perelman.

When Perelman's former father-in-law, Robert Cohen, died, Perelman sued. He sued claiming that his former brother-in-law, Jimmy Cohen, the son who worked in the business, unduly influenced his father to transfer shares of the company to Jimmy. By the time the business was sold, Jimmy owned 80% and the father owned 20%.

Perelman maintains that if there was no undue influence, more of the business would have been owned by the father than the son, Jimmy. Perelman's expert testified that had all of the transactions been fair and had not been unduly influenced by the son, at the time of Robert's death, Robert's estate would have been worth $450 million more than it was. And that the only reason for the $450 million to have not been part of the estate was Jimmy unduly influencing his father.

I testified that I disagreed with that position, the calculations, and with the premise that there was undue influence. Our client Jimmy Cohen won his case. He did not have to pay any part of the $450 million due in large part, as written in the decision, because the Judge agreed with my testimony.

CHAPTER 9

PAUL SCHAFHAUSER

Paul: My name is Paul Schafhauser. I'm a litigation partner at Chiesa Shahinian & Giantomasi. I practice both in New York and New Jersey in the state and federal courts. I specialize in several areas including real estate litigation.

Before I practiced in New York and New Jersey in federal and state court I engaged in commercial litigation involving real estate matters, intellectual property matters, corporate divorces as well as other business disputes. I have also been engaged in claims for professional malpractice and other valuation related disputes.

Ron: When you have to seek an expert, where do you look for them?

Paul: I primarily value my own past experiences with experts with whom I've developed a rapport; also referrals from colleagues. Also, I will do a Google search for people who might sound well on an internet site but may not play out so well in an actual court matter. I generally begin the process by speaking to and about people with whom I've worked in the past.

I value referrals from other people that have dealt with a particular issue and who have practical experience with the person who might be a call.

So to put it out in the realm of the specifics and deal more generally, what I do when I'm not familiar with someone in that particular area. In some areas, I will get recommendations from other practitioners and then I will call and have a dialogue with the expert.

I like to have the client on the phone call so that the client can get a sense and be invested in the decision-making process.

Ron: And that's a telephone interview?

Paul: It's generally a telephone interview. When the list is winnowed, I will pick three top candidates and call people that have worked with those experts.

Ron: Do you ever ask for a face-to-face interview? Or can you make your determination based on the referrals and speaking to them?

Paul: It depends on the time pressures involved and also the magnitude of the case. Sometimes I do ask for a face-to-face interview if there's sufficient time and if the dollars at stake warrant the expenditure of resources to arrange for a face-to-face interview. I can avoid the need to have a face-to-face interview if I'm familiar with that person. That's why there is a great comfort working with people that have demonstrated excellence in past matters. I avoid having to go through that process by working with people like your firm that has excelled in the past. It's only in the cases where you don't have someone recognized in that particular niche area where the interview process has to be done.

Ron: What are the types of cases that are appropriate for seeking out a financial expert?

Paul: There's a wide variety of cases. I wrote down some examples and I'm obviously not going to identify clients. I had a matter in which one of our clients was the mortgagee on a property worth in the tens of millions of dollars.

There were allegations of financial improprieties and we retained a forensic accounting firm to investigate to come up with an analysis about what should've been done and where the money went. Category 1 is where a forensic accountant simply has greater expertise about accounting matters and a greater knowledge of where irregularities might be found.

The second category is in valuations. Disputes about valuations are of all kinds, of all shapes and sizes. I have a case in which we have made arguments about the value of a property that is subject to a bankruptcy proceeding. That's the kind of case that I bring to a financial expert, where valuations are an issue.

I have another case pending where we have an installment payment motion under the New York City of Art. I hired a forensic firm to assess the fair value, what time incurred by the judgment debtors under a pretty specific and unique New York statute. That forensic firm came up with an analysis as to value which I felt was very creative.

Lawyers can pontificate as to what they think value might look like. But a forensic accounting firm brings to bear not only a unique experience and way of looking at things but also a level of credibility that legal advocates don't have on their own.

Accounting malpractice is another area where I've had some issues with firms. I am involved in a hotly contested trade secret misappropriation case that involves a number of intellectual property issues.

An IP case is where we have an economic expert that opines the alleged lost profits as to the plaintiff's unjust enrichment theory as well as to what the value of the alleged trade secret would be. Economic experts fulfill a valuable role in a number of contexts.

Ron: Are there certain qualifications that your financial expert must have to be retained by your firm?

Paul: I would say, it's not to duck the question, but it really depends on the kind of case.

In the case that I was just telling you about, the plaintiff had hired a PhD economist. The thought was that if the plaintiff goes in front of a jury with a PhD economist, we would need a PhD economist to counteract it. Not that I happen to think that that degree implies a better judgment on the numbers. A jury may weigh the testimony of someone with that piece of paper differently than that of someone who doesn't have that piece of paper.

I like working with forensic accountants more than with PhD economists because I think they bring to bear more practical experience. PhD economists, in my experience, and at the risk of stereotyping, tend to have a more theoretical background.

All things being equal, if I'm not faced with someone with a credential that I feel like I need to match, I lean toward forensic accountants.

Ron: If the trier of fact wasn't a jury, but instead a judge or a panel of arbitrators, do you feel the same way about matching the credentials?

Paul: No, I don't. I don't think a judge worries about those kinds of issues nearly as much as a jury. And by the way, I don't know for certain whether jurors would focus on that. You don't want to be faulted by hiring someone that a jury might perceive to have a different set of credentials.

Ron: Do you think juries might look at a forensic accountant as a hired mouthpiece versus a PhD economist as having more of their own view, that they're not biased?

Paul: No, I think that with effective examination or cross-examination; the point can be made in front of a jury as to who is paying the bills for whomever the expert might be. I don't think that one or the other is perceived as more biased.

All things being equal, a forensic accountant has a better grasp of practical considerations than many PhD economists. In the case that I was just referring to regarding the trade secret misappropriation case, I was leaning toward hiring a forensic accountant until we found out the other side had hired a PhD economist. We were worried about how that would look in front of a jury.

Ron: It's a fair strategy. You answered my next question which is if you prefer a professor in academia to a professional expert witness to a practitioner of traditional accounting.

Paul: I would go with a forensic accountant. I weigh heavily the expert's experience in having rendered opinions in the past, having sat for a deposition, and having sat for a cross-examination at a trial. It is a factor. An accountant that has never been an expert would be a more difficult sell for most clients than a forensic accountant that is well-versed in the nuances of litigation. It makes a difference, not just for me but also for the clients. I was on the phone with a client the other day and the client asked how many times this person has testified. It's a question that clients want to know the answer from the start.

Ron: In my experience, very few forensic accountants have testified more than ten times. Most cases settle, right? Ninety five percent of your cases settle.

Paul: A lot of cases settle before you get to trial, but you might go to a deposition. At a minimum, you prepare a report. With a number of cases that I mentioned, we didn't get to a hearing or a trial.

The report was rendered, additional analysis was done, and the case either was settled or it went away on dispositive motion practice. That's a fair point. When I say testify, I don't necessarily mean at a trial. It could be at a deposition.

Ron: Do you inquire or does it matter how often the expert has been on the defendant side or the plaintiff side?

Paul: I certainly inquire. It may or may not make a difference depending on the answer to the question. If the answer is something in the order of, "I've been on the plaintiff side 70% of the time and on the defendant side 30% of the time." It doesn't wow me. If the answer is, "I've never testified for a plaintiff and I'm on the defendant side every single case." That answer lends itself to a good cross-examination where someone is making their living solely by defending it. You get the idea.

I've also interviewed someone that had never testified on one side of the issue, but had always testified for the opposite side of the issue. It's something to consider.

On the other hand, if a person is on both sides of the issue, they also can be a problem. You have to do your homework. You have to look at what this person has written in the past regarding the issue in question.

Because heaven forbid, that expert writes an opinion for you and your client, takes a strong, strident position and then the other side comes up with a report or testimony showing the same expert said exactly the opposite. That happened to me as well.

Ron: That being said, do you ask for prior issued reports?

Paul: I do.

Ron: Do you get them because you want to see what their opinion was, to get a sense of their style of writing, and a sense of what their exhibits look like?

Paul: It depends how familiar I am with the person beforehand.

I'd much rather work with known commodities than unknown commodities. Not to call anyone a commodity, but you get the idea.

If I'm familiar and comfortable with someone, we can have a conversation and I will know fairly quickly what I can expect to receive from that person.

Ron: Definitely, that'd be a comfort.

Paul: Right. There is a comfort level and predictability just like McDonalds has made a great amount money. Wherever you are in the world, if you see McDonalds, you know exactly what that hamburger is going to taste like. It may not be the best hamburger in the world, but you know what it's going to taste like.

You know what the french fries are going to taste like, and we all can taste those french fries without even thinking about it because there's a predictability. And so with people that you've worked with already, there is a predictability. I ask for references of people I haven't worked with. Are there lawyers who have worked with these people? I start looking on Lexis and Westlaw to find what their prior reported decisions looked like, expert reports in the past for a sample of what their writing style, and how thorough they could be and will be.

Ron: Are there some essential traits and characteristics that you identify in a forensic accountant?

Paul: I like to work with people that are thorough. I also like to work with people that think outside of the box, who are creative in analyzing issues and situations. People who think outside of the box, in my view and experience, are also good at responding to unpredictable twists and turns in the case as well as to cross-examination. People, who linear in their approach, are dogmatic as to their view, are more susceptible to being blindsided by the inevitable curve balls that will come up in a litigation.

Ron: What are the core skills that you identify a forensic accountant needs to possess?

Paul: First of all, the person needs to be recognized as a well-credentialed and well-experienced accountant. Secondly, the person needs to be able to articulate his or her point of view in a logical and persuasive way. Thirdly, the trait of being resourceful and thinking outside of the box is very helpful in being an expert and the economic expert. Those are the things that come to mind.

Ron: When you see a forensic accountant as ineffective, what reasons can you identify for that ineffectiveness?

Paul: I'm thinking of a matter in particular that goes back a number of years. The client was willing to spend whatever it took, and we had a forensic accountant on the job who was eager and well positioned to make the case. But we didn't have the raw data to work with. We weren't able to obtain through discovery the necessary financial materials for him to review. So he was ineffective because he was not able to even render a report that carried much weight at all. It wasn't because he was an inadequate accountant or expert; it was because the data wasn't there. The underlying information wasn't sufficient.

We also found out that someone had taken a position on the case and this was not disclosed to us. He had taken this position on the opposite side of the issue and then was opining. It made things difficult.

Ron: I can imagine. And that came out in the cross?

Paul: No, it was beforehand. But it's where we're unable to deal with. It was a negative surprise that clients are not enamored with.

Ron: When do you hire your expert? When do you start seeking? When do you retain them?

Paul: There are two answers. The best practices, litigation answer, is the sooner the better. The practical answer is as soon as the client's budget will allow you to give a green light to hire an expert. I prefer to have the expert early in the case, while the discovery is still pending. So that the economic expert can help guide what documents to request you're propounding, who you're subpoenaing, and what kind of questions are being asked during the deposition. it's very helpful to have the economic expert involved sooner rather than later, for those reasons.

Once discovery is over, especially in federal court; courts are very loathe to extend discovery or reopen discovery once it's closed. It's very hard to bring someone on with 30 to 60 days to put together a report. And then to find out that it would've been useful to have asked this question or to have asked for this document or that tax return or that financial statement, only to learn that discovery is over and that question wasn't asked; sooner is better.

Ron: You mentioned that the client budget is always the concern. They're fee conscious, of course. If you don't have to bring on an expert, they likely don't want you to, unless they see the value.

Paul: I explain to clients that just because the expert is retained early on doesn't mean that the expert is going to be spending 40 hours a week on the case. The expert can weigh in on an as-needed basis if an issue arises. But at least you'll have the benefit of having that expert weigh in before it's too late.

Ron: Are there any drawbacks?

Paul: The reality is that the report is going to cost whatever the report cost, whether one does it two months before the close of discovery or a month after the close. Most reports are done after the close of discovery because you might amend things.

Ron: You said you like to bring them on as early as possible. Are there any drawbacks to bringing your expert on early?

Paul: The primary drawback is money. Clients get nervous when they have additional vendors to cut checks to. And even if the checks are small, it requires the client to bring on an economic expert early on in a case.

There is another advantage to having an expert early on in the case. The sooner the expert is able to speak cogently to the issue, the better you'll know your own upsides and downsides, and the attorney and client will be able to evaluate sentimental alternatives more intelligently.

If you want to have mediation early on or midway through the case, it would be very helpful to have an expert on board so that you're not walking into mediation blindly as to what your exposure is.

A good expert will also help assess what you're likely to hear from the other side. An expert will know what I'm going to hear from the other side's expert. What is that person going to say, within the realm of reason?

No one can predict with certainty what someone might opine. But within the realm of reason, it's helpful to know what the worst case is that you might hear in either mediation or a courtroom.

Ron: How do you strategize with your experts? Do you role play as if they were the expert on the other side?

Paul: It's hard to ask someone, but I like to know what that person would say if he or she were on the other side. I like to know the arguments they would be making if they were on the other side of the ledger. What theories would they use to poke holes in our case if they were looking at it from the other side? A good expert will be able to look at that and think outside the box by viewing the case from the other side's perspective.

Ron: Are there any risks and challenges by strategizing with your expert?

Paul: Strategizing in the jurisdictions that I work in is not discoverable because it is subject to the privileges that apply. I'm hard pressed to think of a downside, honestly. To strategizing with the expert sharpens each person's analysis. knowing what you might hear from the other side makes you attuned to the arguments that you'll need to rebut as well as the arguments that you'll need to attack head on.

Ron: How do you develop your discovery requests? And do you ask for your expert's help?

Paul: That goes to the question of how early I am able to bring the expert in. The sooner the better. If I'm able to bring the expert in while discovery is pending, I like to include the expert in the strategizing of our discovery issues. I like to send the expert the deposition testimony as it's happening or as soon thereafter as possible. I don't like to dump a whole bunch of deposition transcripts on the expert after discovery is over because then it's too late to change anything. So if the expert spots something; it's nice to have that when you have the opportunity to make changes.

Sometimes I ask for the expert or the other side asks the expert to sit during a deposition to participate. In some IP cases, experts sat through the depositions of individuals that were likely to speak about financial or damages related issues - officers of the company, CFOs, sales people talking about the sales, causing the lost profits, and that kind of thing. It's helpful to have the expert in the room listening and feeding questions if the question presents itself. It's a cost-benefit analysis.

Ron: How do you prepare your experts for their depositions or during the trial for their cross? Do the more experienced experts get less prep time with you?

Paul: I guess I'm old fashioned and I don't like to take chances. Whether the person is experienced or inexperienced, you have to do your homework. I like to go through the report and role play as the other side's counsel and ask both provocative and probing questions to see how that expert reacts. We then fine tune the responses in the event of trial.

People who have done this ten times are less likely to make rookie mistakes than people who are in fact rookies, right?

Rookies are more prone to make rookie mistakes. But you can't take anyone's testimony for granted. So I go through the report and figure out what questions the other side would ask, what are the weak spots, what are the assumptions that are aggressive and what are the assumptions that drive the analysis. If it's a valuation and at some discount rate is a linchpin of someone's opinion, you can be sure that that discount rate will be open to lots of questions; why did you pick this discount rate or that discount rate.

I focus on the assumptions that drive the analysis because those are the ones that are most likely to be probed as well as the ones that are the most significant because they're driving the analysis. I don't focus on things that won't move the needle so much. Because if that's not going to move the needle that's less likely that people are going to spend a lot of time on them.

Ron: When you're reviewing the damages reports, are there different areas that you can identify that become the most compelling components of the report?

Paul: It's very important to be as specific as possible in the report. And yet not so specific that the expert boxes him or herself in and loses the reader of the report. It's a catch-22. On the one hand, you want to be very specific so that your report is not deemed to be dubious. At the same time, you want to leave some wiggle room so that if circumstances change or if your testimony needs to be modified at trial, you have room to do so.

The other thing that I look for, again, is and this is a judgment call. Is the report and the opinion that's been rendered reasonable? Does it sound reasonable to the ordinary person? Is it comprehensible? Or does it sound too good to be true or far-fetched?

If it sounds far-fetched to me and if it sounds too good to be true, it's probably not going to carry a lot of weight. I make a judgment call as to whether the report sounds reasonable, because those are the most compelling reports. If they sound reasonable, we'll probably be much more complacent.

Every assumption has to be measured by that same reasonable standard. If there's some underlying assumption that is crazy, a good lawyer will smoke that assumption out and the report and the opinion will collapse like a house of cards. If one piece of that little house of cards is pulled out, it's a problem.

A good report not only is thorough and detailed, it appears eminently reasonable. That is the most persuasive kind of report. If the trier of fact reviews that opinion as more persuasive than the opinion of someone who may have the best credentials with the best background but who ultimately is trying to sell a theory, that is unsaleable.

Ron: When you said you like the reports to be specific, what are you looking to see for the specificity? Is that towards the amount of lost profits? Is that the discount rate? I didn't follow which part you want.

Paul: It depends on the kind of report we're talking about, but I'll pick discount rate. If the discount rate is a big factor, it's important to explain why the discount rate is reasonable and appropriate under the circumstances. Whatever factors there might be, whether there's a creditworthiness issue, a speculativeness to the profits, or whatever it is that needs to be explained with some textual support for it for why the number appears as it is.

It's important for the expert to cite what he or she has reviewed, and what assumptions are critical for the report. There needs to be an explanation for those key assumptions.

Ron: When you're working with young associates, do you feel that they have been trained or learned enough from law school as when to use a financial expert, when they see what type of cases require one, and do they know how to use them or is that something that is on-the-job training?

Paul: I think it's on-the-job training. I'm not sure that I had any experience until I worked at the law firm at which I worked in using expert reports in their appropriate way. It comes with experience, like many things in the practice of law. The notion of what will sell in the front of a jury, when to bring on an expert, what kind of expert is most likely to make a persuasive case; all of those things come with experience. We certainly train our associates and work hand in hand with them on how to litigate matters. But there's no substitute for experience and there are no shortcuts to that. It just comes with experience.

Ron: Finally, please share a story or some anecdote about a case you worked on when you have used an expert and they helped you win the case or they didn't; or the other side, where you saw their expert help them or they didn't.

Paul: One case that comes to mind is a case that I mentioned earlier where we have a fairly creative argument under a unique statute in New York for installment sale.

The expert that we hired came up with a very creative analysis of what the judgment debtor's imputed earnings could and should be. The judgment debtor was seeking to avoid paying his creditors. And the expert made a showing, based on the evidence that we had obtained, that in fact this judgment debtor was rendering services for no significant compensation and under the statute was evading his financial obligations to creditors. The statute in New York gives you the right to make an application for an order compelling that judgment debtor to make payment.

That's one case that comes to mind that's somewhat unique, and our financial expert made a very strong argument and showing based on his detailed analysis of the evidence including lots of deposition transcripts, financial statements, tax returns, and other items that we obtained during discovery.

Another instance that comes to mind with a very different kind of expert was a case where we hired an expert to opine as to the legal fees and damages sought in a title insurance matter from the insurer. This expert was able to assess the damages and expenses and fees in great detail, having had experience in that area. And again, I thought, made a very compelling showing that the amounts being sought were excessive.

Ron: What was the result in that case?

Paul: The result is still pending; it's in the appellate courts.

Financial experts bring a lot of skills, abilities, and perspectives. And it's my pleasure to work with them on a regular basis in my practice.

Ron: In your experience, do you see a growth of other attorneys using financial experts or it's pretty level the last five to ten years? Where do you see it going in the future?

Paul: Good question. I think it depends on the nature of the litigation in play. To the extent that IP cases become more predominant, yes. To the extent that corporate divorces become more prevalent, yes.

And by the way, I forgot, for a large part of this discussion, about all the corporate divorce cases where I've had a forensic expert weigh in. That's a great example of a litigation where someone has to figure out how much was earned, should have been earned, how much was accounted for or should have been accounted for. The expert comes in and asks the right question about this account and that account and why the tax returns don't match up with the bank statements and why the bank statements don't match up with the in-house documents.

Those are the kinds of cases where an expert is not just invaluable, but essential. Those kinds of cases are becoming more prevalent; thus, the need for financial experts is becoming, if anything, more significant.

Another unique case involving a forensic expert analysis that just came to mind involves a chain of pizzerias. The chain was being challenged by the IRS for tax evasion because the IRS was asserting that the pizzerias were not paying the appropriate amounts as a predominantly cash business. We hired an expert to demonstrate that the cost of the pizzas, the overhead, and the cost of everything that went into selling products to the customer was just as we had said; we, meaning the chain to settle on its tax returns. We showed that the revenues, when imputed the sales, the revenues were consistent with what the tax returns showed. The client was able to get that resolved through expert analysis, even where receipts were lacking and the government was focused on the lack of documentary evidence.

Ron: Do you know how much value the IRS was asking for?

Paul: It was a very significant amount. This was a number of years ago and I don't remember the specific number. But it was a successful resolution.

Ron: Good. I like to hear those successful resolutions.

CHAPTER 10

WILLIAM SONDERICKER

William: I'm William Sondericker.   That is William F, as in Frank, Sondericker. I am an attorney at Carter Ledyard & Milburn LLP, a New York law firm at 2 Wall Street and that's where we are sitting today.

I'll give you a bit of background on the firm and myself. The firm is an old firm as it began in 1854 with James Carter. I think James Carter was the original partner who started the firm. Of course, he was here long before I was born. James Carter was a prominent lawyer. He was a founder and the first (and only two times) President of the New York City Bar Association of the Harvard Club where his portrait stands in the main hall. The firm has been in continuous practice on Wall Street since 1854. It's a general corporate firm and does general corporate work as well as litigation. It has a highly recognized, nationally known trusts and estates practice. Generally speaking, it is a general practice firm that engages in all areas of the practice of law.

From my own standpoint, I'm an older attorney and I think the oldest attorney in age in the firm. I graduated from law school in 1952 and was admitted to the bar in 1953. I was an editor of my law school's Law Review. And I'm admitted in a number of courts around the country including the New York State Bar which admits me to all the courts in the State of New York. I'm admitted to various federal courts, including the United States Court of Appeals for the Second Circuit here in New York, the Third Circuit in Philadelphia, the Fifth Circuit in New Orleans, the Eleventh Circuit in Atlanta, the Eighth Circuit in St. Louis, the Federal Circuit in Washington, D.C. and also the United States District Courts for the Eastern and the Southern Districts of New York where we have our principal practice.

Ron: Impressive. Which areas of law do you typically practice?

William: My career has been varied and wide. In my earlier days I did a lot of antitrust work and was involved in antitrust litigation from 1952 when I started as a law clerk, after graduating from law school, but before taking the bar exam and being admitted. I think the very first thing I worked on was an antitrust case. And I worked on antitrust cases all the way through the 1990s into the present in Delaware. One large group was the over 1500 electrical cases in 35 judicial districts in the 1960s, more in the 1970s and the uranium cases into the 1980s.

Along the way, I parted from that and did a lot of other things. I worked on product liability cases. I've had some very good success in product liability defense work, especially in the courts in New York and the U.S. Court of Appeals in the Second Circuit.

And I have done work for publishing companies. I have worked for McGraw-Hill, for example. I did corporate work for them one of which happened to be an antitrust First Amendment Reporter's Shield related matter in which our client ultimately prevailed in an appeal that vacated a lower court's contempt of court conviction for refusing to disclose confidential sources. I've worked on civil litigation in many different places both federal and state courts. In federal court, for example, I had a major case and trial in Ocala, Florida years ago.

In the last 20 to 25 years, I've been doing a lot of work for overseas clients. In the last 15 years, a great deal of my practice has been in the area of patents, contracts, licensing and ANDA antitrust pharmaceutical litigation for Japanese pharmaceutical companies.

Ron: What areas of specialties do you believe are appropriate for a financial expert?

William: That's a very broad question and it requires a very broad answer. There is practically nothing that is in litigation that, in some way or other, will eventually not require some kind of an economic or a specialty in what we call liability and damage analysis. For example, in medical malpractice, you're going to get into damage experts, the doctor's analysis, that sort of thing. In eminent domain, expert land value and use analysis is needed.

In securities litigation, which I've done a considerable amount over the time, it's almost always necessary to have an economic expert appraise the value of stocks or a claim involving the loss that the plaintiffs have suffered or damages that they have claimed. And also that the defense disputes and both sides will have economic experts to testify in that respect. I have also used those experts in tax cases. We also need to retain accounting experts at the same time, because many of the very good experts are in the accounting field. They are usually CPAs and also other degrees in the accounting area that their specialties are accredited in and give them the qualifications that enable them to testify as experts about economic losses and damages that the companies or individuals or defense counsel need to explain why they should or should not be required to pay damages.

One thing I didn't mention is in the antitrust area, for example, almost always economic experts are used. The economists and accountants, each of whom will have an area in which he or she is specialized and knowledgeable.

The economists are especially qualified in what we call market studies and in opining as to what a particular market is. This is very important in antitrust litigation because the market will comprise those products which are competitive with each other. In a broad sense, the most famous case that started all of these was the cellophane case back in the 1950s. Du Pont was the defendant and successfully defended a government case which alleged that Du Pont had a monopoly on cellophane. The defense was cellophane was not the market; flexible package wrapping was the market. And the defense made that defense stand up.

This brings us back to what I said originally, the economist will testify from an expert's standpoint as to what the market is, what products have cross elasticity of demand with each other in a market that makes them competitive with each other and will affect the price - up or down - of a product if there's a greater demand or lesser demand of one or the other that affects price.

Ron: Are there certain credentials that a financial expert must have for you to retain them?

William: Every expert, in order to be a qualified expert, must withstand original scrutiny on the witness stand or in preliminary motion practice that he or she is qualified to testify to the particular area in which the expert supposedly is an expert. The first thing that one looks at in cross-examination of the other side's expert are the degrees and qualifications. Are you a biologist? Are you a scientist of some kind? Are you a medical doctor? Are you an economist? What degrees do you have? Are they Bachelor degrees? Are they Masters degrees? Are they PhDs? Many of the economists today are PhDs. They'll come from MIT, from the University of Texas and so on.

In addition, they should have some practical experience in the field, of what I would call application of economics to the business world. If it's a securities case, they ought to have experience in the field of finance and marketing of securities so that they know what they're talking about and can answer questions, especially on cross-examination. There's nothing worse than to get an expert on the witness stand that can't answer a question because of lack of knowledge. The knowledge should be broad on the specific topic in which they are supposedly an expert and called as an expert.

And the same is true of accountants. Accountants should be CPAs and many accountants have a lot of other different qualifications. For example, a damages expert that I use frequently has four or five different qualifications of an investigatory nature that qualify him in many different areas such as appraisals of companies, fraud prevention and detection. Accounting principles applies to losses and claims for damages, including defense of same. That is just one and there are many others.

Ron: Do you prefer to have a professor - some academic type - or a professional expert witness or practitioner of traditional accounting?

William: It depends upon the type of the case. If there's a case that involves, let's say, construction. I recall a case that my firm and I were in years ago that involved reinforced concrete runways for aircraft that had to be torn up and taken away from farmland. The land was required by the lease to be restored to its original condition. One would think that it would be a very good idea to have a real estate expert to testify about the value of the land before and the value of the land after and what the differential is with and without the concrete which has to be removed.

In addition to having the real estate expert, one would want a construction expert. Somebody who knows about bulldozers, about heavy equipment, about what it takes to rip up reinforced concrete, what it costs to carry it away and one who can give clear and straightforward answers that will reach a jury or a judge. An expert who can convince the fact finder, who is the jury or the judge, what it is in the real world for a construction company to perform this work, which the real estate expert may know nothing about. So a little bit of both can help.

Ron: Does it matter how many times your expert has testified for the defense or the plaintiff?

William: That's a very good question and there probably is a digression of views on this. Personally, it doesn't matter to me. The expert is qualified if he is clear or she is clear; if the expert is knowledgeable and has a conviction of experts' opinions and the basis on which the opinions are based so that those opinions can be set forth in a straightforward and clear way so that the fact finder can understand them. That the expert is credible is important. Then it doesn't matter because the credibility of the expert will carry the day. In recent patent infringement case our expert on validity of the patent (an engineer/university professor) testified for the first time as an expert and literally blew away everyone. Our damage expert on the other hand had testified many times.

If the expert is inclined to be a little bit wishy-washy, I wouldn't want to use the same expert over and over because the credibility may not be there. The other side will cross-examine the expert and bring out that that expert has been used four, five, or six times by the same firm and that he or she is a professional witness. The credibility, therefore, is not to be believed as being very credible because they do this as a business, as a profession.

It goes back to the qualification, the character, and clearness and credibility of the witness on the stand. If the witness is a good one, no problem; the witness can testify ten times for the same firm or the same individual and it should be fine. That's my view.

I'll give an example of an expert that had great knowledge in an international marketing case. I was in a case involved with the defense and the other side was putting forth a model that was based on half of what was the alleged market. They were trying to extrapolate from that half what the other half was or should be for damage purposes which would double the amount that was involved and would have led to a very large verdict.

The damages expert that I had was a professor at NYU Business School, an MBA professor. He was extremely credible and knowledge in international marketing. He gave forth an opinion that was ironclad and destroyed the argument that the other side was making. That was because "A" was this way which is the basic foundation of their case; "B" which was the extrapolation should be the same way. And he gave the reasons why that wasn't so and why one couldn't extrapolate to "B" from "A". He's a great expert, so it can be done. We won the case.

Ron: When your expert is ineffective is it due to that lack of credibility or for other reasons?

William: One of the major things I have seen that has been the downfall of an expert on the witness stand is being caught with a lack of knowledge in a particular area. Calling a securities expert who is giving an opinion about the value of a company in, let's say, the construction field. And this person is an investment banker with several degrees and qualifications in the investment banking world as well as experience in investment banking. He does a very good job. And then the $64 question comes out of the blue - have you ever represented a construction company? Dead silence.

"Did you hear my question? Have you ever represented a construction company?" "Well, no but...."

It's lost right there. All the rest is lost. It's important to have the expert with knowledge of a particular area in which the opinions are based. Even though he may be perfect for securities and appraisals, a lack of knowledge in a particular area can be very damaging.

Ron: At what point in your litigation do you hire or retain your expert?

William: Well, I'd say in both places towards the earlier stage and towards the latter stage. One of the big factors from a client's standpoint that the law firm will represent is cost. The later it is, the better it is from the client's standpoint because they're not faced with the continuing obligation of paying expert fees while the case is going along. The downside of that is that the earlier the expert gets called in, the more you might get out of them.

The expert can be an advisor and help in the preparation of the case whether for the defense or the plaintiff. And at the same time he can draft the opinions that are going to be used.

From my experience, the experts are hired somewhere about two-thirds of the way into the case, well before the end of the case. It certainly is not in the last two weeks, but it isn't at the very beginning. It's usually well into the discovery and the latter part of the discovery stage. At some point, I think the light dawns that we had better get an expert in here to help out as to where we're going to go with opinions - expert opinions.

Ron: Do you see that trend changing - that more litigators are hiring experts earlier or hiring later?

William: I really can't say I've seen any trend. I think it's a very good idea to get somebody in very early. I, for one, am not as worried usually in the beginning. I'm more concerned toward the end. I would probably alert an expert that we may be using the expert and that the areas in which we may want coverage. But to start the meter might be somewhere down the road a little bit because I'm very concerned about the cost from the client standpoint. The client has to pay the bill and they're usually very worried about running up extra fees that they don't have to pay for at that moment.

Ron: Will you tell me a little bit about how you strategize with your experts?

William: I don't know that there's any general way to do it. It depends on the case. I can tell you a couple of cases that I've worked on in the past and that I'm working on now. The basic idea is to understand what the basic principles are that we have to get across to the fact finder - the judge or the jury. And what it is we're trying to show as the theme of the plaintiff's case or the defense case. And then have the expert come in and say here's what we're trying do.

For example, right now, there's a patent case that we're involved in, in Texas. We're about to hire what I would call, not an accountant or an economist, but rather a demonstrative evidence expert; somebody that prepares PowerPoints and that sort of thing to show. This case involves a lot of technology, biology, and bioscience. And so these things are hard to get across.

What we're doing is telling the experts that prepared these PowerPoints what we have and are showing them the patents and so forth and explain what we have to tell the jury. We've got to show them the patents and explain what they do and how good they are. At the same time, we have to show where the defendants have their technology and why their technology infringes on our technology. We need to do this in a demonstrative way so that there's a picture. The picture will make more sense to the jury than somebody speaking and saying "We do this and we do that and the defense does this and they do that". By showing a picture and saying, "here's what we do and there's the step that they do and that infringes what we do"; they'll see that.

This is the strategy we do. We try to get the two concepts in parallel, namely the picture and the concept that is in the patents and put them together to help them to understand and present it that way.

Economic strategy? In a market study, one tries to describe to the expert what the product is; who the competitors are, whether it's national or international; most of the time it is U.S. What the competitive products are, what our client's product is, to whom they sell; what the pricing is - is it high or low? What's the differential between competitors and our own clients? Then we ask the economist to tell us what the market is. We think we know what the market is, but the client thinks we need an economist to strategize what the market is, what products are in the market - are there any other products in the market that we don't know about that may be competitive or that were sold in the market. We want the economist to come up with a market study that puts all of these together so that it can be presented in a block to the judge or the jury.

Those are two examples. The first one is the antitrust; the second is a patent.

Ron: When you're developing your discovery requests, do you work with your expert to develop them?

William: Not ordinarily very much. I suppose on occasions that might be useful. One time years ago, I did. It was extremely helpful because it was an accounting matter and my expert knew better than we did where the bodies might be buried and what to look for and to guide us about what to ask.

In accounting cases, it probably can be very useful to have an accountant to help. Unless you have an accounting background yourself, the accountant can detect things and discrepancies that the ordinary eye would not see. He can also give clues and guides as to areas of inquiry that the ordinary eye might not see.

Ron: This is a broad question. When you're reviewing damage reports, what do you find most compelling about the experts' reports?

William: One is sources. What are the sources and basis for the opinions that are rendered? Two, the clarity with which the opinions are stated. As far as the writing goes, whether it's verbose or clear cut. I do not like verbose writing, from my own standpoint. I'd like it to be short and straightforward so that there is no mistake as to what the intent is.

Ron: Do you ever ask an expert for a report that they've previously issued so you can review their writing style?

William: No, I've never done that. I do talk with them beforehand and get a view as to what I think. That gives some pretty definite ideas. If I think it's not going to work, I come to a pretty quick conclusion and the answer is no, I'm not going to use this person.

Ron: How do you find your experts?

William: There is a variety of sources. One is word of mouth. One expert that comes to mind is such a clear speaker in getting his opinions across verbally. He was word of mouth. Somebody recommended him and I interviewed him and was satisfied. He was excellent and has been ever since.

Another way is there are numerous, especially true of economists, think tanks - Cambridge and so forth. They are a small group of almost like head hunters that run these places and have a roster of professors on their list who are available. Many of them are professors from places like MIT and other business schools. And so you can go to one of them.

For example, the Analysis Group that I've used. They have a list of people that are economists or whatever particular areas you want. They're very expensive. And I tend to be choosy and careful about the way I pick the expert because I don't like to just get somebody that's in there and it gets cost prohibitive.

This has happened to me over my objection. I had a case in Chicago once and it was recommended to me that we use this particular professor from the University of Chicago. He was an accounting expert, but boy, he was expensive. He spent a ton of time on his own just going through studies and whatnot that I felt there was no need for, but there was no stopping. He just kept going ahead and did it. And that's the way it was. I don't like that. I'd rather have more control over the way the case is going to be prepared and the choice of who's going to be used.

There are other groups that specialize in supplying experts of all kinds. There's one in Philadelphia that can give you a list. You can go through the roster and get résumés; then have an interview and decide whether you want this person or not.

Most of the time I use people that I know personally or people that I know who have used an expert. I will talk to them and ask for a recommendation. Then I will interview the expert and say yes or no.

Ron: Do you always interview the expert before?

William: Always. And it's not a five minute interview. I spend a lot of time talking with the person. I've got to be satisfied that this person is clear and has the knowledge. Most of all, he's going to look good and prepare well and be good on the witness stand. This is very important. He has to be able to withstand cross-examination; that can be deadly.

For example, I was in a big case on the West Coast and I was not the principal trial counsel. I was an adjunct person assisting in the case, but I was a senior person. I was called upon by the people that were in charge of the case to do a mock cross-examination of the economist who was going to be the chief witness for the client at the trial. I went out to the West Coast and spent about a week there. They assigned a business person from the company to me and produced a bunch of documents that were relevant. I spent a week or so with this business person learning what was involved and listening to the business person.

On a Saturday morning in a setting that looked like a court room, I was called in. The economist who was a PhD and professor from the University of Texas was there as a witness. I was to cross-examine him in a mock cross-examination and prepare him for trial. He didn't know who I was and I didn't know who he was. It was a totally strange atmosphere as though it were real. I was prepared well because I had a good businessman who was feeding me information.

We went at this for about an hour, and the lawyers who were defending the witness stopped. Why? The witness was being destroyed because the cross was too heavy. He was not a good witness on cross-examination, at least at that point.

That story has stayed with me forever. The witness has to be able to withstand cross. The forensic accounting expert I was discussing earlier is one of the best I've ever seen on cross. The other side rarely can make a point on cross with him. He always has a good answer and a smile and it makes a big difference. There's no acidity to him or to his demeanor. It doesn't look like I'm trying to put you down, but he has perfect answers. He always knows how to handle cross. With cross-examination, you never know what's coming. That's where a witness on direct can be hurt. A good cross-examiner can box a witness in. I need somebody that I feel can withstand a good cross-examination from a good cross-examiner.

Ron: That leads into my next question. When you were telling your example how you practice with the expert, the cross, how else do you prepare your experts for their testimony either in a deposition or a trial?

William: It's done in stages. Initially, one goes through the basic part of the case that the expert is going to be an expert on the facts so the expert knows the facts just as well as I know the facts or the people I work with know the facts. Try to educate the expert or the expert is fully informed on what the case is about and what the arguments are for both sides - the pros and the cons, where the weak spots are, where the strong spots are. So that the expert has a good knowledge of the case - the same as counsel does - so he's prepared.

Then you go into his own or her own expertise - the area of accounting or economics, whatever it is. I hear from the expert what his views are on the case - that this is good, this is bad, this is what we've got, this is a point you have to work on and so forth.

Then we formulate what the theme of the case is going to be. When you think you've got the case pretty well in mind - this is your direct case or defense, then you go into the stage with the expert as to cross to get the other side's view of the case. You have practice sessions of the direct which is easy. We want somebody in the office that is not the same person that's doing the cross.

Then you do the same thing with the cross. Mock cross-examination is very important because you try to know all the questions that the expert might be hit with and that the expert can handle.

Ron: Do you like to have your expert in the room when you're getting deposition testimony from the opposing expert?

William: Yes.

Ron: Do they help you with your questions to ask the opposing expert?

William: It can be helpful if the counsel feels that the expert can be useful. From the beginning, you tell the expert that if he finds something that could be useful, to bring out. Write a note, then stop and then we'll discuss it.

Ron: I'd like if you could tell me another story of a time you've used an expert and how it helped in your case.

William: I've told the one with the professor from NYU and that was about as successful as it gets because there was a lot on the line. There was a lot on the line for a lot of reasons. Our client was a Japanese trading company and we had some language barriers to begin with. It turned out that our client was required to submit marketing reports to the other side, in the course of the marketing agreement that they had together. And our client was marketing the product in Japan. It turned out in the course of the testimony that the manager who was the middle manager in charge of a lot of the selling in Japan, had focused a great deal on one area of the business and one section of customers and, particularly, one customer who had a very large percentage of the business that the client sold.

On the other hand, our client was always nervous, long before we had the litigation. I presume he was nervous about the possibility of being terminated and superseded and the marketing reports were not 100% accurate. The marketing reports spread out the sales rather than focusing on that there were so many sales in one area and not so much in others. While the totals were accurate, there was no misleading in that respect, the spread was misleading. It came out on cross-examination and our person honestly answered and said that the reports were false.

So now back to your question. This led to a bifurcated hearing on liability with the three-panel arbitrators holding that our client was liable for breach of the marketing agreement. When you're liable right up front for breach of contract and maybe fraud going into the damages side of the trial, you're in trouble ordinarily. I mean, it's very hard.

Now I'm set with this was my perspective. I have to defend against the damages theory which was, "although we have been doing all that we were supposed to do in this other half of the business, we would have made way, way much more money," says the plaintiff, "than we made." Our damages were already in the $30-35 million area.

So then I got the international marketing expert and he convinced the three arbitrators that that theory was bunk. It was just a figment of the counsel's and the other side's imagination that they could have sold that much. In part he was saying, in our own self-interest, our client's own self-interest; if they could have sold it, they would have. That's a simple answer. That's one answer, but there are others that the marketing expert was able to put together and convince the panel that the arguments that were being made that we should have had all these damages were untrue. We wound up with a damages award that was hard to believe. We were going to lose because they've already found liability. What was the verdict? One dollar. That was it. We lost $1.

That's an amazing result. But the marketing expert was very crucial. We had two other experts too. One was an accounting expert, but the marketing expert, with his marketing study and model, was key.

Ron: Yes, that's a great story. Once you lose and you moved to the second prong for the damages, you know your client's liable and now you worry about what the panel will determine damages are. Damages will be somewhere between $1 and $35 million, and it was $1. That's a fantastic result.

William: The client was very happy, as was I. When you're facing that kind of an award, you don't know what it's going to be. It can be $10 million or it can be $5 million; you just don't know because it's very amorphous. The theory was that they breached the agreement. They didn't do what they're supposed to do so don't let them get away with it. You have to come up with something that compensates for that loss. That's the argument. And the other argument is, well, there was no loss. It's a hard sell.

The professor is still there. He was one of the leading MBA professors in International Marketing at NYU in the MBA program.

Ron: My last question and then anything you want to add please feel free.

Do you find that the young associates know what a financial expert is or when to use them, or do they need to get educated about that?

William: There are two answers to that question. Number one, most of the young associates are very well schooled on the law. And there are cases in the courts, the Frye case in the state court and the Daubert case in the federal courts, for example. They are what we call the gatekeeper cases or threshold cases where the court has to make a determination at the threshold or at the beginning as to the qualifications of the expert even to testify about the area in which the expert is supposedly qualified to testify. If the court finds after voir dire or preliminarily in motion practice by the other side in cross-examination that the expert doesn't have the qualifications or that the subject matter doesn't bear expert testimony for the client that is being offered; they can disqualify him. Not all of that answers your question. Most all of the associates that are in litigation, if they're out of school any length of time, will know about these threshold cases and know that experts have to be qualified.

The next stage focuses on how to use an expert, what are they supposed to do, and the strategy. Some of them will have an idea. It depends on what the subject matter is. If it is something like a market study, they may not be really up on it. But if the associate was an Economics major in college; he or she probably has a pretty good idea. If they were an Accounting major, maybe they don't. If they were Biology or Chemistry major, maybe they don't. On the other hand, if they were Chemistry major they may have a pretty good idea about the patent case I was talking about earlier because so much of it is bioscience.

So, yes and no. You certainly don't want to rely 100% on the associates. It takes a lot of thinking to put together how the expert is going to present the case in a way that is going to be clear, convincing, and credible.

Ron: I think that sums up a lot of what you've said what you look for in your expert.

William: Clear, convincing, credible, and have the knowledge to apply to the case and be strong on cross-examination. That's right. Those are key things.

Ron: Yeah, you summed it up pretty well.

CHAPTER 11

SETH TAUBE

Seth: I am a senior partner at Baker Botts, an international law firm. I am Chair of the firm's New York litigation section and Global Chair of the securities litigation practice. My practice is commercial litigation with an emphasis on securities litigation, SEC and regulatory defense, white collar crime, foreign corrupt practices, investigations, and corporate governance.

I've practiced for 35 plus years, having begun my career as a prosecutor with the Securities and Exchange Commission. I was promoted to Branch Chief of Enforcement and then went on to the U.S. Attorney's Office in the Southern District of New York. I was an in-house counsel at an investment bank for a short time and I've been in private practice since. My cases have tended to be more international and are significant litigations, investigations, or disputes throughout the United States, Asia, and Europe.

Ron: This book is about how litigators win their cases using financial experts. How do you find your experts?

Seth: My approach to experts is different from other lawyers. What I need first and foremost is someone who is convincing on the stand and can react well to cross examination. Testimonial skills are more important than substantive expertise. At the end of the day, an advocate's job is to convince the jury or judge of the truth of your position. The presentation of each of the factual and expert witnesses, the manner they speak, how convincing they are, and that they can demonstrate depth of knowledge in cross examination is what is critical. Substantive skills are important but secondary to testimonial skills.

Ron: In order to discover if they would hold up against the cross examination, are you typically using people you've used before or do you use referrals from other people in your firm?

Seth: One develops one's own network of trusted experts in each area over the years. You'll get referrals, initially. You inherit experts as you mature as an associate. Ultimately, you need to become comfortable with these people. Lawyers are constantly bombarded with lunch invitations, party invitations, dinners, vacations, whatever it takes to get hired. I've often found the best experts, best at testifying, best substantive knowledge are not at the largest shops but at boutiques. You're looking for the personality in the testimonial skills as well as the substance of their knowledge

It's like clients: it's developing relationships with people you trust and who have stood up over time. Once you find someone who's good on the stand, you tend to go back to them as long as they can qualify as an expert in the relevant area required.

Ron: What are the areas of specialty you believe are appropriate for a financial expert?

Seth: First and foremost, experts on damages. Those are the most important. Many lawyers focus on liability and do not spend the time and energy on damages early in the case. Getting the right expert early on is critical: coming up with the right theory, and pursuing the documents from your adversary to support the damage expert's needs. As such, there is a need for damages experts early on. Most lawyers think, "let me get a liability expert and I'll worry about damages later." That's a mistake. Damages come first because many cases are won on damages and not on liability.

I had a very large matter in China involving the country's largest telecommunications manufacturer, either the first or second largest such manufacturer on earth. The case had problems with liability. It had to do with a dispute between the Chinese company's manufacturing and equipment and the Canadian plaintiff's endeavors to operate a South American telephone network involving equipment in South America and Miami.

There were issues on liability, but we won the case on damages. It was an international arbitration. The claimant sought $4 billion in damages. Regarding liability, we put up the best case we could but there were issues. The arbitration panel awarded $2 million out of the $4 billion requested.

Again and again, you see cases for plaintiffs won on liability and lost on damages. The biggest issue lawyers overlook and the most important thing to add to the team early on is a damages expert.

I had another case recently where I was consulted on the plaintiff's side. They had a slam dunk liability case but a very weak damages case. The case wound up getting settled because the other side focused on the damages issue.

What skill sets are important? A financial expert that understands valuation of businesses, can look at financial statements, financial books and records, look at a set of facts and come up with rational, scientifically accepted theories for compiling or minimizing damages.

Separately, you need liability experts. Those experts have to have substantive knowledge in the specific area of the business at issue. If you have a mortgage backed derivatives case, there are a series of people you can use out of government, Fannie Mae, Freddie Mac or the Inspector General's Office. So sometimes you get someone who's had a fancy title from government for liability.

If I had a choice between two experts; one who had a national reputation in the substantive area, another who knew the substantive area but was better on the stand, I pick the latter because what counts is what comes out of their mouth.

Ron: Are there qualifications that you always seek in a financial expert?

Seth: Putting aside the testimonial capability, what I need is not only substantive knowledge but an ability to think outside the box or take a set of facts and construct strong financial arguments. Just as I'm an advocate of the law and the facts, I need an expert to be an advocate of his substantive area. A great expert, like a great lawyer, marshals the facts, applies them to his area of expertise and comes up with convincing arguments to build his case.

            An expert is an advocate, even though he or she is deemed an independent expert. Once hired, he's an advocate in his substantive area just as the lawyer is on the issues of law.

Ron: Do you prefer if your experts are in academia or if they're a practicing CPA or if they're a professional expert witness?

Seth: It depends on the nature of the issue. We have some matters which are of first impression; there you need an academic because they've thought about hypotheticals in the way practical people have not. Usually someone with hands on experience is better than an academic. But I'm giving you an example of where that wouldn't be the case. You need to be flexible.

            My default position is someone who's done it rather than an academic. For example, the Chief Accountant at the SEC, who is a good advocate, now winds up in private practice. I could see using her as an expert on accounting issues. However, if someone is a CPA for many years in some local region and is better at testifying, I would go with them.

Ron: Do you inquire or does it matter how many times your expert has testified for the defendant or the plaintiff side?

Seth: You always try to find people who've testified for both sides. Ironically, people seek out the testimonial virgin so that they don't appear to be leaning one way or the other. But for the reasons I've expressed, that's a mistake. You need the testimonial veteran. As a result, it's always good to see people who've been on both sides.

Not because it matters on their analysis or the quality of what they do, but it's one less thing you have to worry about on cross examination.

Having said that, there are some areas of expert testimony where there is a plaintiff's bar and a defense bar. The classic example is in securities class action damages. There are certain people known as plaintiff's experts who do the damages calculation one way, and defense experts do it the other way. Because there are two different techniques - the plaintiff's version of how to measure damages and the defense version - it's hard to use someone who's done both because they are contradictory.

Ron: What are some essential traits or characteristics you've identified with a good forensic accountant?

Seth: Facility with different types of financial presentations is helpful. Often you come up with damages theories or liability issues out of the box. Not everything fits a financial statement. I need someone who is facile with different ways to compile damages, different avenues or theories, using different sources. Sometimes the key source of evidence isn't available, so you need to build around the hole in the evidence and build a case anyway.

I need experts who are facile in all different types of financial data - financial statements, valuations, cash flows, whatever. I need an expert who can come up with a theory and then link it to existing professional publications and accepted data so that he can pass a "Daubert" type expert test on the quality of his work. ("Daubert" is the Court precedent mandating that experts must demonstrate scientific acceptance of their theories of liability or damages.) It must stand up against accepted accounting and other financial standards. Most importantly, someone who can think on their feet. If presented with new facts and new evidence, someone who can work through it, around it, or turn it into an asset.

In other words, a great expert is able to look at a difficult set of facts and make a silk purse out of a sow's ear. Yes, there are all these bad facts. But, if you look at them this way, it's actually better for us. That's what great lawyers and great experts do.

Ron: Do your experts ever use demonstratives?

Seth: Demonstratives are wonderful. In an era of electronic capability, every trial lawyer comes to a court room with a laptop and a series of demonstratives to summarize the facts and expert testimony. Because experts tend to be in exotic or less understood areas of human understanding, it's critical for them to be able to simplify complex concepts. That's one of the key elements of expert utility beyond testimonial and substantive ability, to simplify the complex. If they are an expert, it must be a complex something to be an expert about. A financial expert needs to be able to simplify.

If you have the ability to explain what a derivative security is to a jury or how market data is compiled by the New York Stock Exchange or how some obscure industry generates money; that's a key quality. In all things in being an advocate, less is more. The ability to use a demonstrative and simplify complex facts to a simple chart, graph, or picture is by far more effective than getting into the weeds with the expert and the jury.

Ron: What are some core skills you identify for your expert to possess?

Seth: If it's a financial expert, vast experience, understanding and learning in accounting. A financial expert must understand different financial products, business models and business modeling, and valuation.

Ron: When these financial experts are ineffective on your side, or the other side; will you identify some of the reasons for that ineffectiveness?

Seth: There are two or three things I worry about with an expert. First, if they take a position that's too firm and absolute, then the smallest chink in the armor can bring down the entire construct. You need an expert who is careful never to set forth absolutes to stay out of trouble.

You need an expert who is not going to fight all aspects of the case. If you're a damages expert and the damages expert is asked whether liability exists, assuming that question is allowed to be asked, the answer is, "I'm assuming liability in order to come up with damages." Do not fight battles you don't have to. Don't be dragged into areas outside your expertise. Often someone who is an expert in X will give a report that goes into X and Y. By exceeding your area of expertise, you'll undermine the entire endeavor.

I've seen cross examination where the expert is testifying about liability and damages. It turns out he doesn't know a darn thing about the underlying industry, so he's unable to testify on liability. Experts will also sometimes attempt to testify up to the ultimate issues of whether the case should be won or lost. This is subject to objection and is a mistake.

Those are some of the areas you can get into trouble with experts. Like everything else in testimony, less is more. Focus in on four or five important things. Do not use the expert for fifty different things because you're going to have weaknesses, lack of expertise, or incongruities which will get you into trouble.

Ron: When do you retain your expert? When would you like to? Is that different than when you actually do?

Seth: I like to retain experts before the complaint is filed to help come up with the theories of liability and damages. Clients inevitably don't want experts brought in until later. There is a typical tension between the pocket book of the client and the desire to win of the litigator to get the expert in as early as possible. Sooner is better because it helps filter what discovery you seek, how you approach your own proof in the case, what documents you want to get from your clients.

Ron: When money is no object, they're brought on before any complaint is filed?

Seth: Yes. When money is an issue, if you have a relationship with the firm or the individual, you can usually obtain some free advice from the expert with the promise that if the case gets far enough they'll be hired. You have to honor the promise or you will only get to do that once. You ask for some free work early on, to brainstorm with me for a couple of hours and then down the road you get hired. That's usually the way you can solve the problem.

Ron: Are there any drawbacks by bringing in the expert early on?

Seth: Occasionally, the assumptions the expert brings to bear prove wrong with the facts and you have to re-jigger things down the road. But that's rare. Lawyers, like businessmen, make decisions based on relative risk and it is much less risky to bring an expert in sooner rather than later. Things can always go wrong. You can bring in the wrong expert and come to the wrong conclusions because the facts are incomplete. Therefore, you've gone in the wrong direction. But nine times out of ten, going early to the substantive expert in the relevant areas, particularly financial expertise, is well worth it.

They don't teach accounting in most law schools or, if they do, it's a quick course on the basics. Occasionally, you'll get lawyers who are CPAs just as you get Intellectual Property lawyers who were doctors first. It's usually a mistake to play accountant, to play financial expert. Lawyers aren't bankers or accountants. Draw on those with expertise, draw on them early, and it will make a huge difference in the success rate of your matters.

Ron: A couple of questions on strategizing with your experts. Is that something you do?

Seth: Always. You have a core team, a brain trust in every litigation.

Your brain trust consists of the lawyers, the key spokesperson for the client, an in-house lawyer for the client if there is one, and your expert. That team needs to talk before filing, and at each major step in the case. Sometimes decisions along the way about what discovery you seek, what questions to ask in a deposition are significantly affected by the input of a financial expert. You won't know what questions to ask otherwise.

I've had situations where I'm going to question someone over a financial statement so I look to the experts to provide some original views. I show my outline of the deposition to the expert if I'm deposing a financial expert on the other side, or deposing a CFO, or an accounting person. They can help build the questions so that the answers put the deponent into a corner from an accounting or financial point of view.

I view a financial expert as the key member of the team every step of the way, including jury instructions. If you're going to ask the jury specific questions, it has to be a question sheet for them to answer yes or no. On the financial matters, have the accountant involved because there is some key language which will protect you on appeal.

Ron: Are there any risks or challenges to bringing them on as part of your brain trust?

Seth: As I indicated before, each expert - the lawyer on the law, the accountant on financial issues, and the client on the business - each of them could come with prejudices, misunderstandings. But, from a relative risk standpoint, including your financial expert early on in the brain trust is much more likely to be positive than negative. The answer is, on a relative risk basis, it is an easy call.

Ron: You mentioned you like the expert to be involved in the jury instructions. How about discovery requests?

Seth: Particularly with financial discovery, the expert helps you draft the questions. Historically, there was an issue between a testifying expert and a consulting expert. At least federal law and many states now allow you to shield from discovery the consulting pieces of the expert's advice. You have to look at your state law to see whether you need a consulting expert and a testimonial expert.

Ron: When reviewing damages reports, do you ever ask your experts for previously issued reports just to see their sense of writing, or to know what their exhibits look like, or for any reasons?

Seth: The previous work by the expert is critical because it's often subpoenaed by the other side; it's a subject of cross examination. You need to see their previous work. Prolific experts have dozens or sometimes hundreds of prior reports; the way to parse through that is to say I need reports of this type within the last 5 or 10 years.

You get a sense of whether he can be cross examined if somebody finds a report from an earlier matter. With the advent of electronic access to court filings, there are services that can get you the testimony as well as the filed reports of your expert in every prior case. All of that is online and available through databases. The miracle of the internet is: one, there's no privacy; and two, experts get cross examined in ways they never had before. You need to see that because the other side can get it whether or not they get it from you.

You want to look at prior testimony, prior reports. With the onslaught of available data online, it is not so much whether you look at it but how you discriminate what you want to look at and what you want to ignore. You need to make decisions of what type of prior testimony and expert reports that your expert has done are most likely going to be either the subject of cross examination or support of the positions you're advocating.

Ron: What makes an expert report compelling?

Seth: The expert report itself, unlike the testimony, does not need to read like a Tom Clancy novel. It needs to be a legal brief in the expert's area. You need an expert report that's not so much reader friendly as it is authoritative. You need theories laid out by evidentiary support, charts and graphs. Most importantly, you need an expert report that picks the important two, three, five issues the expert is opining on and sticks to those. Less is more once again.

You need to vet it with the expert, and to do a little cross on it before you publish it to the other side to see where the weaknesses are. Often the expert will tell you: "here is where there is thinner factual support or support in the literature; here is where there could be weaknesses". You can discuss that and be prepared to work around it or live with it. But the narrow approach of a report is what's critical. Don't take on more than you need to.

Ron: What makes an expert report compelling is very different than what makes for compelling expert testimony?

Seth: Precisely. The report is a vehicle for cross examination. The testimony is a vehicle for convincing the trier of fact of the truthfulness of your position. The report needs to demonstrate expertise that will defend the Daubert challenge and a narrow but convincing position based heavily on the literature in the accounting or financial field.

Ron: How do you prepare your experts for their trial testimony? And is that different than for deposition?

Seth: Depositions these days are commonly videotaped. There was a time when written transcripts didn't require a witness to be visually friendly; as long as the written word looked good you were fine. With videos, whether you're testifying on the stand or at a video deposition, you're essentially testifying on the stand.

That change in practice, due to technology and the inexpensive price of video depositions, means that preparing the witness for the deposition is the same as preparing him or her for trial. His or her answers need to be concise, authoritative. He or she needs to be user friendly, not hostile, not obnoxious. He or she wants to demonstrate to the questioner that he or she wants to be helpful in explaining his or her position without being patronizing. There's a real art to it. The key point is that there's no difference between depositions and trial anymore for the reasons I've expressed.

Ron: Do you prepare your expert for cross examination differently than you would prepare a fact witness for cross.

Seth: Yes and no. Both need to not be hostile or argumentative. It shows that you're trying to be helpful in uncovering the facts through the expert area. There are commonalities to testimony in making a good witness. But beyond that, the expert needs to have a mastery of the area sufficient to be able to respond based on authoritative accounting literature, financial literature, damages literature, and the like.

Don't bite off more than you can chew. Answer the question directly; that's true of any witness. But an expert has the additional burden of explaining his position. An expert is expected to be somewhat more lucid and detailed in responding to a question than a fact witness.

The fact witness answers only the question asked. The expert is an advocate. When given a window to be able to present the broader theory of damages or liability, one of the key differences is to have the expert take the opportunity to repeat some of the key points from direct on cross. An expert can get away with that. A fact witness shouldn't try.

Ron: When you're getting ready to depose your adversary's expert or to cross examine them, do you use your financial expert to prepare for that? And if so, how?

Seth: It starts with the receipt of the adversary's expert report and obtaining from your expert all the avenues of attack, all the weaknesses, all the problems with their theory, with their numbers, with their calculations, with their reliance on inappropriate accounting or financial literature. You often have them sit with you at the deposition of the adversary's expert. You have them sit with you at trial during the adversary's expert's direct testimony to make sure your expert adds any last minute questions before you cross examine them.

When confronting adversary experts, your own financial expert is the equivalent of your co-counsel and your closest and most important consultant in dealing with them. They are an extension of your own ability to bring this case to a successful conclusion. The closest working relationships you can have with your expert is their assistance to you in attacking the other side.

Ron: If you could, please tell me another anecdote of a time you used an expert and it worked well or it didn't go well. Or the other side used an expert that went well or didn't go well.

Seth: I recall a trial in which we had an expert. On direct, she gave a broader opinion than she had the expertise to support. She went from damages to liability. She said why the other side's financial situation was handled inappropriately. On cross examination, it was demonstrated that she didn't have the expertise on this particular area of accounting practice to be able to opine on it.

She said, for example, at this company in the accounting department, there should be someone that looks over invoices looking for X. On cross, it was established that the role of accounting, approving invoices is based on a set of procedures to ensure quality in compliance. What she was proposing the company's accounting staff to do was not standard practice anywhere in the industry. That significantly hurt her substantive and qualified opinions on damages when she had ventured into a non-damages area.

That would be an example of why you have to vet and train your expert to testify only on what they know and not to go off the reservation. Most experts understand this, but some want to be helpful and get into the spirit and emotion of the case, and try to be more useful. That makes them less effective.

Ron: Finally, do you find that young associates coming out of law school understand how to use financial experts? Do they understand when they would need them, when to bring them on? What advice do you give them?

Seth: Some young lawyers have experience in accounting or financial matters or in the financial world. But the vast majority, yours truly included, came out of law school without a clue on how to read a financial statement. I had no sense of how business worked, but had a very rigorous understanding of the thousand-year law of property from England. It's a classic mistake thinking being a lawyer makes you smart in all matters.

One thing young lawyers can do as they come in contact with financial experts in their practice with senior lawyers is to ask the experts if either they or people on their staff would sit down with them and spend some quality time, sometimes on the clock, usually not, explaining how things work. Use financial experts to teach you how financial statements work, how finance works, the present value of money, the Black Scholes Theory of valuing options. Teaching the next generation is both an ego boost for the expert and a service of what you do as a trained professional.

Use your experts and the staff of the experts to help train the young lawyer. We all need to learn and become facile in an ever complex financial world: understanding the body of literature, rules, and financial concepts that are encountered every day as a trial lawyer of commercial cases.

Don't assume you're an expert in all things. Don't assume you can learn it yourself. You have a real benefit in sitting down with experts and letting them talk to you about how their universe works. Absorb it. Over the years, you will become much better at figuring out the cross examination question that will win the case.

Ron: Great. Those are all my questions. Do you have anything else you want to add?

Seth: I think these were a great set of questions in terms of understanding the issues. The final comment I'd make is chemistry is important. You need to like your financial expert, spend time with them. Understand when you can and can't use them because you need different experts in different areas.

Personal relationships enhance both parties in being unafraid to raise criticisms, objections, thoughts, and suggestions. You should develop a relationship with your expert so you're both open to talking with each other when either thinks the other is going off the cliff. Thanks.

Ron: Great. Thank you so much.

CHAPTER 12

JANTRA VAN ROY

Ron: Please introduce yourself, your firm, what type of law you practice and then we'll get into the questions.

Jantra: I've been practicing in the same general areas since 1990. I have primarily represented banks and other financial institutions as secured creditors in a variety of courts and a variety of types of disputes. I have focused over the course of the decades on insolvency-related matters including bankruptcy cases large and small where my client is usually the primary or a primary secured lender.

I have done lots of real estate based insolvency work representing the mortgage holder restructuring loans either on a consensual workout basis or a less consensual bankruptcy basis or in straight up litigation over a default in the lender's rights.

I also do regular, it's probably not regular to most people, but regular asset-based loan default work. When a bank is owed on a working capital line or some such things secured by inventory, receivables, equipment or other assets and the business is failing either on a balance sheet basis or a cash flow basis, the loan is in default.

173

I have always viewed litigation as an expedited settlement track. As is true with any time one tries to resolve a dispute, leverage or get closer to what might be an imposed outcome by a court can get the parties closer to the same number.

This firm ZEK (Zeichner Ellman & Krause LLP) primarily represents banks and other financial institutions, although we represent many other businesses and other facets of commercial law both transactional and litigation. Your focus is on our litigation practice so I speak for myself. I would be shocked if most of my litigation partners didn't see the world of experts in the same general way I would.

Ron: My first question is: how do you determine where you seek your experts?

Jantra: I would prefer always in person but it's not always feasible.

Ron: What are the areas of specialty you believe are appropriate for a financial expert?

Jantra: I've used experts to assist the fact finder in understanding issues in many types of matters.

Ron: And what are the qualifications you seek for in your experts?

Jantra: The expert needs to have a certain amount of well-recognized expertise in the field to testify. I've been talking so far about testifying experts. If we talk about a non-testifying expert to get to serve as part of the litigation team and provide guidance, then the particulars on the résumé are less important to me. But the résumé needs to be there.

            Beyond that, there are two general views as to what qualifications are at the top of the priority list. Depending on who the fact finders are in the matter, either view is sensible. I have a particular leaning towards the second. So let me describe the first.

The first view is someone wants an expert that has a "bowl them over" kind of résumé. For example, he's on 18 national committees, has four degrees at Harvard and speaks at Yale every month. The fact finders will be so impressed by the credentials that they might not understand what the expert is saying. But, they'll think to themselves, "Well, he or she must be right because of all those fancy degrees."

The other approach, which I favor, is that one always has to look at the specifics of a matter and who the audience is. But I favor, all else being equal, an expert that can explain to the fact finder what's going on and the reason my argument is right or the reason for my result is that what I'm off pitching for is right.

An expert that knows his material and will convince the fact finder by laying it out in a way that the fact finder, whether it is a sophisticated judge or a less sophisticated juror, can understand and nod along. And in essence, say, "I see. Of course we have to divide that in half and then we have to multiply by 0.8 because of taxes." And then if we can get the fact finder doing that, we often nail the issue.

Ron: Do you prefer an academic, a practicing CPA, a professional expert witness?

Jantra: The best combination with which to impress a fact finder is normally a combination of stellar academic record, whether the person is in academia now or not, and some practical experience. It's wonderful if the person is not a professional expert witness because that tends to cut a little bit into credibility in the eyes of many fact finders, but that's rare and hard to find and not imperative. I focus less on the spectacular academics and more on the practical experience, but there are lawyers who see that very differently.

Ron: Do you inquire and does it matter how many times the expert has worked on the plaintiffs' or the defendants' side?

Jantra: I would put that question differently. Unlike many other areas of the law such as tort law, for example, my clients are both plaintiffs and defendants.

It does not particularly matter to me whether the expert has represented borrowers or lenders, which is more in tune with my lingo. I would play up the fact that my expert has frequently represented borrowers and made a very similar analysis he's providing in my matter on behalf of the lender. That gives additional weight to the testimony and lends credibility to say, "What this is about is the right analysis of the income statement", for example, as opposed to the borrower should never have to pay fees or some such silly argument.

Ron: What are some essential traits or characteristics that you can identify as being important for your financial expert to possess?

Jantra: Any time one is hiring a professional, one wants the professional to be responsive and available and does not whine when something has to be done overnight. And it's not unique to experts or to accountants. It's just what one expects of a professional. My clients expect them rightfully so of me.

I am personally enamored with traits that make it easy for me and, therefore, easy for my client and presumably easy for a fact finder to understand what the expert is saying. My antenna goes up negatively when an expert is unable to explain something to me in simple lay English. When the conversation can't be had without lots of multi-syllable, technical words, I worry that the expert doesn't know what he's saying or he will be unable to explain it to my fact finder.

Ron: What are the skills that you tend to seek in an expert?

Jantra: The two primary skills go hand in glove. They are inexplicably intertwined with each other. The two skills are that the expert understands what the case is about and, you notice, I did not say what my case is about. One of the key roles of the expert is to help me understand counter arguments and the weaknesses in the positions I'm taking. The expert has to fully understand the legal issues and then the factual information about which the expert is going to opine and can explain that back to me and presumably back to a fact finder in a very clear way that gets all of us saying after each couple of sentences, "Ah! So now I understand." I look for someone that can get a stranger to the matter to say, "Ah! So I see." That's critical.

Ron: Albert Einstein has a famous quote, he said, "If you can't explain it to a five year old, you don't understand it yourself."

Jantra: I did not know that quote but that's what I'm getting at.

Ron: When have you seen a forensic accountant or a financial expert be ineffective, what are some of the reasons for that ineffectiveness?

Jantra: I'll give you some reasons and I'll also give you a very funny story about a case that, someone you know, was involved in with me. I see several reasons which overlap with each other for ineffectiveness. The use of very technical terms that none of the fact finders who are listening will understand is perhaps not the reason for the ineffectiveness, but it's a sign that the expert will be ineffective.

If the expert doesn't understand his audience well enough to realize that that audience is not following along, we have a problem. Unless that lawyer wins the lottery and the audience says, "Well, he's got a lot of fancy degrees, so he must be right. I don't understand a word he's saying, but it's okay." I don't rely on that kind of luck. In a competition with someone that has perfectly acceptable degrees and someone with a million fancy degrees, the better explainer will win out.

I've seen what I think is the cause of ineffectiveness, but one very rarely knows what's in the mind of the fact finder. The story I am going to tell you is an exception. I think a huge portion of the ineffective testifying experts simply don't understand what their own trial team and their own side's litigation position is. They are opining about all kinds of fancy stuff, but missing the point a little bit. To me that says they have not been working closely with the lawyers as a part of the trial team. Rather – and again, this is an overlapping reason – they felt that they knew everything and they didn't need a bunch of lawyers telling them about the case. They think they know exactly what the financial statements mean and they can just tell the world. It goes a little bit to ego which sometimes overlaps with the million fancy degrees on the résumé. As you can see, I have a very strong personal bench; other lawyers will tell you differently.

An instance in which I got that rare glimpse as to what the fact finder was thinking about the other side's experts involved in a case – it's public and what I'm referring to is part of a published opinion – the Louis Frye company had three testifying experts. Your dad was one of them. He was retained by my firm on behalf of Merrill Lynch Business Financial Services, a Merrill Lynch group, to testify as to damages in the case involving a competitor coming in and stealing our borrower's service business. That borrower was in bankruptcy so that trustee also hired an expert to testify on the same issue. We had a cool strategy because Merrill Lynch was only owed X millions of dollars and beyond that it wasn't Merrill Lynch's problem, and I was retained to represent only my client.

We were able to use your father to provide a very salable, not pushing the envelope, analysis as to damages that would get Merrill Lynch paid in full plus a little more. That was a very conservative way to view the damages. The trustee put on an expert that pushed the envelope because the trustee represented a much bigger constituency and that expert testified that the damages were even bigger than Mr. Rosenfarb said because there was another way to look at it. That was great and we worked very closely together so that they did not contradict each other. It was simply that the judge could go either way.

And finally, the company accused of, I'll say, stealing, but the technical term is converting my client's assets wrongfully, had an expert, a big shot of sorts. He was one of those with the drop dead resume. He testified that there were no damages because the company couldn't possibly have been saved, so there was nothing there.

There were a couple of funny stories about that expert that came across as a big shot, his résumé in support of that, but as unlikable, because he was not explaining anything particularly well. One story occurred at his deposition, where I knew – based on the tone and tenor of the matter – that he would testify about his own history and experience in a very pompous way; which he did. This was well over a decade ago but as I recall it, he testified at the deposition in substance that he had almost single-handedly restructured the steel industry in this country. That was the implication. So I then asked him, "Wow, if you can do all that, are you really saying that you couldn't possibly have figured out a way to turn around this little Louis Frye printing company?" He was forced to do a "humunah-humunah" because he did not want to admit that had he been called in earlier that he couldn't possibly have restructured this little printing company and created some value which meant damages if the business was stolen.

The second story occurred on the stand and in the decision. In my view, this expert took the same tone, had not learned his lesson from silly me, and had the same approach on the stand. This was a bench trial. The judge was a very sophisticated bankruptcy judge in the Southern District of New York, was used to fancy résumés and did not need to have it explained to him like a five-year old.

He was the type of audience who could absolutely understand the highfalutin terms. In his decision, the judge said, I can't quote it because I'm not reading it but I'll summarize it for you. The judge said that the expert's testimony was in effect "unencumbered by any analysis." In other words, just saying I have 18 Ivy League degrees and I say the damages are zero, doesn't make it so.

And I think that quote says a lot, judges rarely tell you why they didn't buy an expert report. By buying I mean, fall for it. They often pick at particulars within the report and those are all legitimate comments, I'm sure. You know, this factor or that equation didn't work here for the following reasons. But ultimately, what's going on I believe in their mind is much bigger picture. Either the guy made sense or he didn't make sense or he was an ego maniac who thought he didn't even need to explain it to me because he has enough degrees I should believe in him. I think that's really what's going on in the judge's mind.

Ron: And that leads to the ineffectiveness?

Jantra: That's pretty ineffective for a judge to say your opinion was unencumbered by any analysis.

Ron: When do you retain your experts? At what point?

Jantra: My preference is as early as possible in a matter where I see the need to convince someone or put on evidence for things like valuation or lost profits or projections or impairment of cash collateral or whatever it is. The reality is, our clients have budgets, cost is a big issue and I need to have something more to support a request that my client pay for an expert early, something more than my general thinking that is a good idea.

Ron: Are there any drawbacks to bringing in an expert early?

Jantra: Mostly cost and because you can get tunnel vision. When you bring in one expert that has a particular view of a matter then you haven't given yourself room now that he is onboard as far as the trial team to play out other ways of looking at it.

Ron: Do you have experts you can just pick up the phone and call to discuss the case without retaining them?

Jantra: Yes, and I do that. I expect that the folks on our roster will be more than willing to let me pick their brain here and there for matters in which they have not been retained. One of the reasons I have that expectation is because we provide that service to our clients. We expect that any of our financial institutions or other clients can pick up the phone and use our firm almost like a help desk. It doesn't have to be on a billable matter before we'll answer a question.

Ron: Do you strategize with your experts? If you do, how do you go about it?

Jantra: I tell the expert the story of the case and explain what my client's goals are. Unlike tort law and other areas of the law, the goal is not to get as much money as possible. When one is representing a lender, the lender is only entitled to get repaid in full. In full might include late fees, legal fees and other things, but we don't normally get punitive damages. It's important to understand the goals so that the expert doesn't go crazy about theories that might be a little less salable, but could result in a massive recovery. If I'm only out $3 million, I don't need an expert that will push the envelope and risk the credibility of my matter or position by trying to get me $10 million, because I can't keep it anyway.

Ron: Do you work with your experts to develop your discovery requests?

Jantra: Yes, I prefer to. I would prefer always that by the time I'm doing discovery that I have a clear theory of the case which is subjective to massaging based on what the discovery reveals. I would hope that the expert could help pin down what I need to establish my case.

Ron: When you review damage reports, either from your side or the other side, what do you find to be most compelling in those damage reports or expert reports in general?

Jantra: It would be the same thing as in the oral testimony, a clear analysis as to why the theory or opinion being presented works and the support for it.

Ron: Do you ever ask your potential experts for previously issued reports?

Jantra: Almost always.

Ron: Is that to see their sense of writing, to see how they organize?

Jantra: It's everything because we can do a report differently than the way they used to do it. If I don't like the way they packaged it or the way they wrote that can be dealt with. It's to make sure they'll be credible because their reports are out there and available. I don't want someone asking why they said the opposite things just last year.

Ron: When you prepare your expert for a testimony either deposition or a trial, how do you prepare them?

Jantra: I do not prepare for a prep session normally though there will be some prep sessions. I usually work very closely with an expert on a case. After we've been sitting together throughout the matter, then we do a more formal prep session where I play devil's advocate. I pretend to be my adversary and try to poke holes in the case. We will do a summary dry run, depending on how big or complicated the matter is of the direct testimony. That's pretty traditional, but I don't usually end up face to face for an extended period of time with my expert right before he testifies.

Ron: When you are about to depose the opposing expert or cross them, do you ask your own expert to be there for the deposition?

Jantra: Normally, I do. That's a budget issue. It's always preferable.

Ron: The young associates that you work with, do you find that they have knowledge regarding how to use a financial expert or when they would use them?

Jantra: I find that the thing they need to learn most, assuming the budget permits, is to make the expert part of the team rather than feeding the expert the three opinions we need and asking the expert to package up the following documents to support that. To develop the legal strategy together to begin with makes it easier for everybody and makes the story consistent and logical and, therefore, salable.

Ron: Thank you very much for your time today.

CHAPTER 13

WILLIAM WALLACH

William: My name is William Wallach and I am with the law firm of McCarter & English. I started here in 1989 and became a partner in 1994. My primary area of practice is what is referred to as business litigation which has two components. One is business contract disputes and the other is a specialty in disputes involving family-owned or closely held businesses and corporate divorces.

Ron: How do you determine where you find your experts?

William: It truly depends on the nature of the case, the nature of the judge; I will come back to that. And even early on if I have a sense that it is a matter that could settle sooner rather than later, or if it is a matter that is going to go all the way to trial. Because that is going to have an impact, are we trying to impress someone now to resolve the case or do I need to focus more on an expert. There are a lot of qualified experts. I focus on an expert who I think will have the best rapport with the judge. I do very little work in front of juries that involve experts. There is not one general answer as to how I find the expert. It really is case specific.

Ron: Will you talk a little bit about what you meant when you said that you want your expert to have the best rapport with the judge, how do you judge that?

William: You see it in a few ways. It is something that I always work with the expert on. And that is to try as much as you can to make eye contact with the judge when you are testifying. That is the best way of seeing if your testimony is being received. Is it going over the judge's head or is it somewhere in between?

Another way of trying to find out if there is a rapport is when the judge starts asking questions. I encourage the experts I am using to work into their testimony, "Judge, if there is anything that you want to ask about, certainly let me know while I am testifying", or "Judge, I know that I went over something that is somewhat arcane for those of us who do it professionally, do you have any question about what I just said?"

That is what I mean about developing a rapport. Some experts are better at it than others. I also know there are some judges that do not want an expert looking at them. They want the expert looking at the attorney asking them the questions, which poses a different challenge.

Ron: What are the areas of specialty that you believe are appropriate for a financial expert?

William: Subject to your editing, I would say, the lack of b.s., first and foremost. Nonaccountants believe that accounting is black and white. Therefore, an expert accountant, an expert financial investigator, a financial planner, or whatever the expertise is, needs to speak unequivocally. The hemming and hawing, saying things that sound great, just do not work. You have to be candid. You have to know your stuff. There are a lot of people out there who know their stuff.

It is going to come down to what is the most effective way of communicating that expertise. Is it going to be at trial or is it going to be early on as I said in the context of settlement where you want to impress the other lawyer and the other client? So that they think, "I do not want to go on trial against Wallach and his expert."

Ron: What are the qualifications you seek in your financial experts?

William:	Let us use the example of a valuation of an entity. I am not willing to have that expert qualified as an expert for the first time on my client's dime. They need to have testified before. And they need to have testified before for at least two reasons. One, I do not want them choking on the witness stand. Everyone is nervous when they testify but you are less nervous if you have testified previously. If you have never been subjected to direct or cross-examination in a real setting before, it is going to be a new experience and your expertise and your knowledge may get lost in the presentation.

Another reason, and related to that is, if you have testified before and your testimony has been accepted, you do not have any skeletons in your closet. If you are testifying, you know, making up numbers here. But if you are 45 years old and testifying as an expert for the first time, on cross-examination you are going to be asked, "how come no one ever used you before?" No matter what the expert says in response, the judge is going to be thinking the same thing.

I know you have to testify the first time once, but it is not going to be with me. The money is too great for what is at stake. So that is certainly an important factor - experience.

Going back to what I said a moment ago, you have to know your stuff. It is not a matter of if have you published enough articles or if you have you spoken at enough seminars. I have my own views on that, whether that is just padding. It is whether you have a mastery of the area and you can communicate it. I know a lot of smart people. But the ones that impress me are the ones that can take their knowledge and make it understandable to others. That is another important quality that I look for in an expert.

Ron:	Do you prefer or does it matter whether you are using a professor, somebody in academia, versus a practicing CPA versus a professional expert witness?
William:	I have had one very bad experience with a professor because the professor was not giving direct answers. The professor was being somewhat ivory-towerish. This was a real life situation with real

litigants and real money involved, and the expert was hired to advocate neutrally. But to advocate for my client, not to pontificate, which was what the expert was tending to do. I will probably never use a professor again.

And in a nonfinancial situation, we used a professor as an arbitrator in a case. Both sides realized it was a disaster while it was going on. We needed someone that was unequivocal and decisive. The professor/arbitrator seemed to want to make everybody happy which made everyone unhappy.

Ron: Do you inquire or does it matter how many times the expert has testified for the plaintiff or the defense?

William: In the ideal world that does not exist, it would be nice to have an expert that has testified for both the plaintiff and a defendant. Focusing on the work that I do, particularly the disputes in closely held businesses, when there is a complaint, there is often a counterclaim. So the label defendant or plaintiff does not really matter. What matters most, and what judges like to hear is, okay, you testify whether for the plaintiff that might be a shareholder or for the company. What did the judge in that case determine? Did he find you more credible than your adversary's expert or not? That matters more than the label.

At the end of the day, it is someone that is taking their specialized knowledge trying to educate, you know, us idiots about what all the initials mean, what all the principles mean because they do not make sense.

Ron: What are some of the essential traits or characteristics that you look for in your experts?

William: I like experts that speak in plain English. I know that they are light years ahead of me in their knowledge so it is the ability to communicate clearly. Because these people are very intelligent, have a breadth of knowledge, and are confident. I find more so than anything else you will win; whatever winning may be. You will win with the expert that the judge is the most comfortable with.

The expert that the judge understands and who is not just taking an extreme position because he or she is being paid by the litigant.

So to that point an expert who will concede that the buildup should have these series of numbers which are more in the middle than an extreme, is going to get a lot of credibility with the judge. And judges appreciate that. An expert was supposed to be a true intelligent neutral and not just a professional expert that testifies to get his or her fee.

Ron: And you said earlier that you want your expert to be more credible than the adversary's expert.

William: And understandable.

Ron: And understandable, good. What are some core skills you identify, that you look for in your forensic accountants or financial experts?

William: First and foremost is the ability for me to understand what they are saying. If I am not going to understand what they are saying, it is very difficult to ask them questions during direct examinations that will elicit answers that a judge is going to understand. They have to be able to communicate.

It is helpful to have the various degrees and certifications because there is no need to have to explain why you do not have them. It shows you took the additional classes and you passed a certification test. They are like shoes to me, you just need to wear those. But just because you wear them it is not enough. It matters to me how I think this expert is going to appear. There are a lot of very smart people out there, but if they cannot make their point clearly and concisely, their point is not being made.

I will tell you because the case is done anyway and I can tell you more of the details. Four or five years ago I was involved in a very bitter dispute over the valuation of a company, I had an expert who I thought was absolutely wonderful. I still think he is wonderful. He was on the witness stand between direct and cross-examination for a day and a half. When he finished, we still had more to do that day so I did not get the chance to talk to him when we left the court room.

When I called him that night to say, "I just want to tell you that you did a wonderful job." He cut me off saying, "Oh, I know that already." I said, "okay. You seem pretty down to earth and not full of yourself so okay. Why are you telling me that?" "Because you guys finished right at the lunch break, you stayed to work. I am walking to my car and I actually saw the judge in the parking lot. And the judge complimented me and said I just want to be clear about one thing you testified to."

It was a complete ex parte communication. But what the expert said, "yeah, the judge started by complimenting me and the judge did understand what my answer was." And in the decision we then received about eight months later, our expert was accepted 100%; the other side's financial expert was qualified, and was practicing for 20 plus years, and his views were found not credible.

Ron: When you've seen an expert be ineffective either that you work with or your adversary, what were some of the reasons for that ineffectiveness?

William: There is an expert that took positions in a case 20 years ago in a Chancery Court matter that were just not supportable. And he would not move off them. If there were six issues he took outlandish positions on all six. The headings of the decision at times indicated, I will leave his name out, but X unconvincingly claims this. He was excoriated by the Chancery judge. People knew about it and it affected his reputation.

What the expert needs to do is say to the client or the attorney is, "I cannot testify to that, I am dead on cross-examination. And if I tried to prop up that argument, it is not going to work. The judge is going to know it, the other lawyer is going to have a field day for it with me and I am shot on everything else." It is better to acknowledge the weakness or concede some points along the way. There are times when lawyers need to turn down cases. There are times when an expert needs to say "I cannot say that," "I will not say that." Their reputation should matter.

Ron: When do you hire your experts?

William: The experts will always say not soon enough, that we are putting too much time pressure on them. But it truly depends. In state court, the rules are much looser as to when you have to disclose your experts and when the reports have to be provided. In federal court, you have to disclose experts earlier which requires you to think more. You have to think more about how I am presenting my case or how am I defending my case.

It also is going to depend upon, where am I seeing this case going. If it is one of those cases where the money is just so much or the parties truly hate each other so much that we are not settling and it is going to trial, then the need for the expert can get pushed off a little bit. If it is a case where both parties think it can be resolved, hiring an expert earlier can benefit both sides.

And to that point what I have been doing for the last few years, which I find very effective, is in situations where the parties believe there is a possibility of settling sooner - agreeing upon a joint expert. This way we do not have dueling swords there. What you have is a process where both sides have vetted an expert, have agreed it is not binding for purposes of a settlement effort, but you do you have this neutral person. And I know from the times I have done it, the experts have loved it because they are not beholden to anybody.

That is an ideal situation. It still requires the clients to then come to terms and agree on a settlement. But that is an instance where you hire an expert right near the onset.

Ron: Are there any disadvantages or drawbacks to bringing in an expert early on?

William: I have not found them to be disadvantages if it is done properly. Meaning, you have to, as the lawyer, clearly confirm in writing whether or not the joint expert's report is admissible in the proceedings if there is no settlement. But there is not a hard and fast rule for which way I would go on that. You do not want to be in a situation where a joint expert has undertaken an analysis, issued a report and it is unfavorable towards your client and the other side gets to use it later on in the case. You have to be careful in deciding on the use of the joint expert's report. Is it just for settlement or can it be used later on in the case?

Ron: Do you strategize with your experts? And if you do, how?

William: That is a tough one because there is no privilege in communications with the expert. I will never put anything in writing to an expert that I would not be comfortable with the other side seeing. I will talk through what is requested for an expert report. I will talk through the expert's views and conclusions if he/she is preparing an expert report. I do not ask for drafts of the expert report because I do not want to have to produce the draft and final version. It is pretty clear in the final version what reflects changes made by counsel, not the expert. So you will not see items like that in writing.

Strategize? Yes, in the sense that an expert is also very helpful for purposes of discovery. What information do I need to seek from the other side? What documents do you need in order to prepare your report? So in that sense, yes. But again, it is a fine line because I recognize there is no privilege as to those communications. As much as I am trying to get the professional knowledge of the expert, I am very careful that if the expert is deposed there is nothing that is going to come back and haunt me or the client.

Ron: Do you ask your experts for previously issued reports?

William: Not always. But what I always will say is, "is there anything I need to know that will not go over well on cross-examination?" And even before I ask that question, the beauty of all the different search engines, you can see where someone has testified before. And you can see what the court has said about his or her testimony. You cannot always get their actual expert report but you can see how the report was graded. And I like it when the expert tells me "I have testified in the following case. And yeah, well, I did not win but the court still found my report credible. It is just...." And I am like, "yeah, I know that. I have read it." I mean that type of situation.

I start off with the background analysis of an expert who I do not know even before I make the phone call.

Ron: When you're reading an expert report either for your side or the opposing side, what do you find most compelling in expert reports?

William: I will say this delicately, what I am using experts for is a subject matter above my pay grade. So what I am looking for is something that passes the initial smell test. Does this sound feasible or does this sound like someone who is just results oriented? Then when I read it for a second, third, fourth time, okay, what is the basis for this? Show me the exhibits or the appendix to the report so that I can see the best data that is out there that will support the expert's conclusion that this officer should have been paid $640,000 a year. Or for this type of company based on its SIC code, these were proper levels of charitable contributions.

When I see the format then I have greater comfort that the conclusions are going to be recognized and accepted by a judge. I am not someone that will say, "The cap rate should have been 16% as opposed to 19%." That is not my area and that is malpractice for me to do it. What I work on is saying to the expert in advance, "when you prepare your report, recognize everything you conclude is subject to challenge, you have to back it up. Every sentence does not require a footnote in the paper. But it does require something you can point to when you are questioned."

Ron: How do you prepare your experts for their depositions?

William: Experts are not always deposed. That is what is interesting. In a situation where expert reports are submitted simultaneously or even if the plaintiff gets a report, a defendant's expert's report, and then the plaintiff gets a rebuttal.

It is not always that you want to depose the expert. I do not want to preview for the other side what I am going to question their expert about at trial. I have an expert that is going to tell me, "yeah, she made a really good point in her report" or "oh, she missed the fact that there is now case law that talks about tax affecting this, so she is completely wrong." Or, why do I want to say to them in a deposition, "how come you did not address the Baustic case" or any other case?

I find that I take fewer expert depositions now because there is not a need to. My own expert will tell me the strengths and weaknesses of the other side's expert report.

But to prepare my witness if he or she is deposed, the analogy I use is like getting ready when you are at bat in baseball. You are on the on-deck circle, you are swinging two bats. So when you are up there, it is easier.

I have yet to have an expert complain to me after the deposition that he or she was not prepared, that there was a topic they were not ready for. There is always going to be a question that no one has thought of. Not because it is outlandish but you miss things, but never a topic. Because you go through their report and try to find the areas where the other side needs to challenge it and needs to probe it.

With respect to experts, whether it is testifying in a deposition or for trial, it is getting them comfortable with the whole process – how to answer questions, not to be intimidated, not to feel the need to fill dead spaces of air by talking. That is how I prepare someone so that they are ready for their deposition, so they are comfortable. They are smart, they know what they wrote, I can help them with the process.

Ron: Is it similar for preparing them for cross?

William:	It is similar. The difference is in cross-examination in court is that you have a judge looking at you. Being deposed, you are in someone's conference room. It is all in the transcript, black and white, with no intonation when someone's reading a transcript. Cross-examination in the courtroom requires a lot more preparation.
	The judge will see if you appear nervous or hesitant or equivocating. You do not want that. I do not care if my witness froze up afterwards when they are done. I want the expert to look like a sphinx while testifying, to be confident and assertive. Not to make things up, but to be confident, which means I do not prep them the night before because that does not work.
Ron:	Do your experts help you if you depose the other expert or about to cross the other expert?
William:	Absolutely. I will speak with my expert as to what my goals are and areas that I thought I was going to go after the other expert with and I will say, "tell me your thoughts as well. You tell me what Revenue Ruling I should ask him about. You tell me why the various factors that they use may be incomplete or inaccurate."
Ron:	Will you share a story with us about a time when you used an expert or you saw another expert and things went great or didn't go great?
William:	Let us start with the good. I am trying to think of experts gone bad. I have not had experts that have gone bad. For an expert going well is, I am going back to the story I previously told you about, the expert that was approached by the judge in the parking lot. If you picture the set up where I am the lawyer, you are the witness and the judge is in the other chair, I am asking my witness – the expert – the questions. But the expert is looking at the judge the whole time and the judge is looking at the expert. I am just like a voice from behind the curtain. The conversation was between me and the expert but it seemed like it was with the judge because the judge was tuned in. The expert was talking right to the judge, three feet apart. The judge felt comfortable asking questions, I would not say interrupting, but asking questions. It was clear that

the judge knew that my expert knew what he was talking about and he was not pushing the envelope, that we were not being piggish. That was a great experience.

That is what I consider a great experience with an expert. In an arbitration which is very different, I had an expert once who was testifying and my adversary actually said to me in a break, "you know, I truly have no idea." I think these were his exact words, "I have no idea what the hell your expert just said. I do not even know how to cross-examine him. I said, "oh when you are done, I will share my views on his testimony as well." That was an expert that sort of got a little full of himself as he was testifying.

It is a great skill not to have a need to fill dead time in the air. You make your points and wait for the next question. Stare at the opposing lawyer. Do not just keep talking. That expert was talking a little bit. Because it was an arbitration, we were able to take a break earlier than if it was in court. And I told the expert, "just cut it out, just answer my questions. Do not pontificate. Do not make these broad statements."

One of his broad statements made him look pretty outlandish but, fortunately, it was not fatal. The other thing I said to him to transition to being concise. Do not just go from 0 to 60 because everyone will know I told you to stop. Gradually start testifying where you should be and that worked out fine as well.

I have not had a situation where the expert says, "well I do not know" or "you are right" or anything like because that is what the preparation is for ahead of time. How you are going to answer the difficult questions; what did he put in the expert report and if it is not defensible, you do not put it in the report.

Ron: You said earlier that you rarely have an expert in a jury trial, why is that?

William: In New Jersey, the Chancery Court hears most of the business disputes. And Chancery does not have a jury. That is the reason why. In non-chancery cases, oftentimes lawyers will agree to waive a jury because you can get to trial in a year to a year and a half faster. You move up the chain. Because in that situation, you are not trying a case four days in a row. You may get two days, a day off and an afternoon. And I have had in the past year or so one trial that has gone over 19 days; and one that was at 24 days of trial over 3 months. That is what you can do when you do not have a jury.

Ron: Can an expert win or lose a case for you?

William: I do not think the expert can lose the case. We are not talking accident cases where I am dealing with an expert that talks about the quality of the brakes on the truck. The experts I work with are talking about the financial world and are calculating damages and value, not assessing liability. What the expert can do is not be convincing and therefore, the judge being a layperson is more inclined to accept the other expert more.

I do not know if I am being clear but as opposed to a judge saying, "I am going to accept 60% of Expert A and 40% of Expert B." I think judges tend to go all in or all out with experts. So you are not losing the case but you are not helping the client in trying to come up with either a higher or a lower value.

To be even more direct, if the expert supposedly is losing the case, it is because the lawyer screwed up. Either you should have told the client to settle the case sooner or better prepare the expert for testimony. If it comes to a situation where something the expert has said in testimony kills your case, you should have expected it. You should have expected it and tried to plan accordingly in advance.

Ron: My last question is about young associates. When they come to the firm, do they know about financial experts, forensic accountants? Because when I was law school, we didn't know.

William: No. You learn about financial experts by asking others. And it gets more difficult because you know fewer and fewer cases go to trial which means there is less opportunity to work with an expert at trial.

When I started way back in 1987, I did not know the first thing about what to look for in an expert or how to work with an expert. That is the responsibility of a senior associate or partner to mentor the young associate and to let them know, very similar to the types of questions you are asking. How do you interact with the expert? What are we looking for in an expert? When are we picking the expert? How do we prepare the expert? That you learn through osmosis and then you learn by doing.

There is a delicate line where conceptually I can tell you I have never used the same financial expert more than twice at trial. For the very reason, I do not want the other side to say, "oh, good to see you and Mr. Wallach are together again. This makes what trial #20 when you testified for one of his clients?" "Oh, does McCarter and English send you a nice Christmas gift? This is the 15th time you have testified for them."

That does not mean it is for the plaintiff or defendant, it is "do you look like a paid hack?" I am sensitive to that. I do not know when I have used someone for trial testimony more than twice. I have turned to certain experts in the consulting world where they do not have to be disclosed to the other side and they may never appear at any place because they are not issuing a report or a witness at trial. There are some experts I will turn to because I know they are good and I know they can answer my questions. And all of that comes from experience and not being afraid to ask someone what should I do or how do I do it.

Ron: Is there anything that I haven't covered that you think would be important for a young associate to read about on "how you win your financial disputes?"

William: What I tell younger associates is do not try to learn the subject matter.

Do not pretend to be the expert. Be the conductor and not the first chair violinist. Know what you want to hear, know how much practice is required, know what the big picture is. How does the expert's testimony fit into the overall case? Be the conductor. But do not think that you are going to master the subject matter the way the expert does because it does not work. If it can happen then you should not be a lawyer and you should probably be the accountant or the forensic expert.

The other important item is, as much as you want the expert to be concise and definitive, you have to be the same way. You cannot let the expert hem and haw or be non-committal when you are talking about the positions you are taking; to the arguments you make or what is going to be in the report. You have to be confident and say to the expert, "you are not convincing me. In fact, I am not following it."

Again, not so much on the technical aspects but, "you are saying words but they are not adding up, they are not resonating with me, they are not being received." That is not easy to do specifically if you are dealing with someone with a lot of letters after their name, who has been practicing for 30 years and you are a fourth-year associate. But you have to do that because you are representing a client. You are not out to make best friends. You can end up being a very good friend of the expert because of mutual respect but you got to be in charge.

What I will often say to experts because I know they are smarter than I am, is to put yourself in the situation as if you are at a cocktail party and you just met someone and they ask you what do you do. You need to be able to answer that in a manner that they understand not just because they had one or two martinis already. But you need to be able to distill your knowledge, your expertise, and everything that you have your certifications for in a way that is understood.

If you approach testifying similar to communicating at a cocktail party, you will be effective. It is the judge or the jury who must understand. It is not the guy that has been a professor and head of the department for 40 years that necessarily carries the day. It is the person that is effective and communicative. That is something I work on with the experts; I work on it with the people I work with, seeking that end point.

We have been talking about the interaction that lawyers have with the expert, what I neglected to talk about is the client's interaction with the expert. The client is, often if not always, the source of information whether it is background facts, whether it is underlying documents, it probably covers the gamut of what exists of the history and the documentation.

You have to temper the client's expectations. And you have to remind the expert as well that if you just want to come across sounding as if we are entitled to so much money that an armed guard is needed to bring the cash into the courtroom, no one is going to believe it.

If you want to work together and recognize that if this was so black and white there would not be a dispute. People hear things differently than what is actually said. People say things differently than what they actually believe they are saying. And I will tell the clients ahead of time what to expect.

Also, I tell experts ahead of time what they should expect from this client. A lot of it is psychological background such as she built this company 40 years ago and cannot believe her son-in-law is trying to take it from her now. So that is shading her views. Or this guy thinks because he is been running the company all these years that he knows accounting. He does not. Be nice to him when you ask your questions. Be nice when he makes statements that you know are not correct, answer them deferentially but disagree when you have to. But do not just say yes and let him think he is right. That is another important aspect of what I do with experts and with the clients as well. Clients not as much, because clients do look at the experts as the guy that knows everything.

You have to work with your expert to understand the client better so that the expert is not blindsided in saying, "my opinion is derived from the following fact." And then it comes out that that fact is based on what the client believes but not what the record shows. I like the experts that will say, "this is my understanding of the facts here. Tell me where this comes from and tell me what the support is for these facts because I am going to be basing conclusions off of what you are telling me."

I say this tritely, there is a fine line between getting to what the right answer is and advocating for the client that is paying to get an answer. The best experts are the ones that want to win but not at any cost.

Ron: Now you raised another question. Experts provide their own opinion based on assumptions that they believe are true or assume that they are true. How do you deal with those assumptions and you're assuming that your client is providing you with the truth as well?

William: That is a very good question. It comes down to what then shows up in the report. Expert reports will have either at the beginning or at the end a list of all documents reviewed. They will include, when they are taken, deposition transcripts. I do not know if the experts actually read the transcript. But if someone's been deposed, the expert better say, "I reviewed the transcript."

I am not asking the expert to tell me the mechanics of your analysis, but let us talk through these factual underpinnings. I will say, "where are you getting that from?" And if there is an ambiguity, I will say, "you can always point in deposition testimony." If the testimony is not there, then you are not putting that in your background facts because it is not sustainable.

That is how I work on it with the expert. Everything has to be three steps ahead. It is not how do you get to your final set of numbers but how will the other attorney with their expert rebut you. If you make an assumption that is not correct, lawyers are going to have a field day. Because then the next question is, "well, let us see what other assumptions you had wrong here," but you still want the court to believe your report is credible?

Everything has to be, if you are making that assumption, where does it come from? If you cannot back it up, you are not using that assumption in writing.

The process is exhausting because you need to think ahead. And it is very difficult for some people to think ahead. If you have not been in a courtroom, you do not have the experience of seeing what happens on cross-examinations and you do not have the experience to fully plan ahead. The client does not want to pay you to learn how to do your job. So it requires a lot of thinking. When it goes great, it is very rewarding. And it can go great when you have done your job. So as we were saying, it does come full circle.

CHAPTER **14**

JEREMY WALLISON

Jeremy: My name is Jeremy Wallison. I'm a business litigator, meaning, I litigate business disputes.

Ron: How do you find your experts?

Jeremy: When you are at a big firm you tend to send around an email to your partners about the issue. You ask if they have any relationships with experts, or know an expert who would fit that bill, that would be appropriate. That is, for example, how we found your firm. One of our partners had used your firm in an accounting matter in connection with his divorce and we had an accounting issue and your firm was recommended.

You develop a list of three or four experts that you want to talk to and interview further. Then you have an informal meeting where you take the measure of the expert. You're trying to find out a number of things: One, does this person have the kind of expertise that would survive an expert's voir dire, in light of Daubert and Kuhmo Tire. The expert needs to have certain credentials and his/her way of thinking needs to be acceptable enough and persuasive enough that the judge will accept the expert's testimony.

The second is to take the measure of how good is that person in responding to questions, how thoughtful does this person seem. Is it a person who seems defensive; a person who has a total command of the topic? Those are the kinds of things that once you get through voir dire, the jury or at a bench trial, the judge, is going to be focused on. It's an intangible thing.

After you interview three or four, at the end of the day, you choose the one that you think will be most helpful to the case. Assuming, of course, that their rates are all relatively similar, and they usually are.

Ron: You mentioned they need to have some types of credentials. What are those credentials that you would require of them?

Jeremy: It depends on the case. In a case that involved a complex accounting matter, it probably would not go to trial if ultimately GAAP were clear on the topic. If, however, GAAP were not clear on the topic then that might push you towards somebody who has a greater grounding in the theoretical aspects of accounting – sort of the purpose of accounting.

            You might be more inclined to retain somebody who has academic credentials. Somebody that is used to thinking about and talking about and persuading regarding the theoretical aspects.

            If it involves "business usage," like how would a normal practicing accountant address or account for a particular transaction, then you would probably want an expert that has real practical experience. You would want someone that has been an accountant for big clients in this particular area or where those big clients have had this very issue.

            The same would go for finance. I mean if you're doing an M & A transaction, you need an expert for an M & A transaction. I think there you might be, depending on what the particular issue is, you might be inclined toward the academic. On the theory that the fact finder ultimately needs to understand the underlying theory in order to understand what the proper financial result should be.

If instead it's about some value of the company, then you would want somebody who has a real practical experience in valuing companies. You would want somebody with the types of credentials that people would be impressed by.

Ron: Do you inquire or does it matter how many times your expert has been on the plaintiff side or the defendant side?

Jeremy: With experts, there is always a sort of push-pull because, obviously, you want an expert that has testified many times. Because, if that expert's opinion has been accepted by a court in the past, that is a pretty good indication that it would be accepted again. And also, somebody that has testified in the past, he's probably pretty good at presenting him or herself to the fact finder.

On the other hand, professional experts are professional experts and that tends to leave the impression they'll say what their client needs them to. And that is not in the spirit of an expert. You want somebody that is objective.

I would be concerned that somebody who has always been on the plaintiff side would necessarily, right out of the gate, have less credibility testifying for a plaintiff. Somebody who's been on both sides would have more credibility.

Ron: Are there some essential traits or characteristics that you look for in your financial expert?

Jeremy: You want somebody who has an authoritative presence. In terms of a consulting expert, what I have found the most helpful is a really smart person.

I've had cases where the issue in dispute was the insolvency of an entity. Well, you have your testifying expert. But I also need to be able to have somebody to walk me through the underlying spreadsheets and walk me through the underlying financial statements. I need someone that can persuade me as to how those underlying facts inform the end conclusion.

Ron: When you've seen a financial expert be ineffective what would you account for some of that ineffectiveness?

Jeremy: There are people that treat it as a job; people who accept what their clients and their clients' lawyers tell them, somewhat uncritically. That creates an incredible vulnerability in two ways: (a) the possibility that what they are being told is not accurate and (b) they will not have drilled down to the extent that the cross-examining firm will. When either happens it can really be devastating.

That's the feature of people in business saying, "Oh, great! I'm getting paid for this and I'm going to keep costs low. So I'll just do what obviously needs to be done and nothing more."

Ron: Just acting as a mere mouthpiece?

Jeremy: In a way sure. It's your father who will tell you. When he was my expert, I tortured him. I sat in his office for days going over everything and asking "how do you get to here? What is this for? What is that for?" That's ultimately what needs to be done and it results in a much more expensive process but a much more bulletproof result.

Ron: When do you hire your experts?

Jeremy: Almost always too late, which is a real mistake. Because a good expert in some kind of financial or accounting dispute will help you formulate the arguments right from the beginning. If you're on the plaintiff side, that could be very important. You can hire an expert at some point down the line only to learn that there was either a better argument you could have made or that the argument you did make has holes in it. And that's a problem. It's very difficult however to convince a client to start paying for an expert right when the client starts paying for a lawyer.

Ron: Is that ultimately the biggest challenge, the fees, as to when you hire your expert?

Jeremy: Yes.

Ron:	Besides the fees, are there any drawbacks to bringing an expert in early?
Jeremy:	There are privilege issues obviously but, those could be dealt with if you are careful about it.
Ron:	Do you strategize with your experts? If yes, how?
Jeremy:	Ultimately, that's half the function of the expert, to strategize – if what you mean by "strategize" is to formulate the arguments and figure out the discovery that needs to done, then yes.
Ron:	Do you ever ask your experts for previously issued expert reports?
Jeremy:	You should because the other side will undoubtedly see them. If there's anything in those expert reports that contradicts the opinion that the expert is currently taking, that could be very bad. You can always try to distinguish. But again, if what we are doing is trying to persuade and you don't have a very good reason to explain the difference between that previous case and this case, that could be devastating.
Ron:	When you read an expert report either your own expert or an adversary's, what do you find the most compelling in those reports?
Jeremy:	First, if it is not clear, you have big problems. And if it is not well supported you've got even bigger problems.
	Like any argument, an expert report that clearly gives the best argument for the other side and has a persuasive way to rebut that argument is usually very compelling. An expert's report that mischaracterizes the other side's arguments, or that doesn't address it in sober terms, would not be particularly compelling.
Ron:	How do you prepare your experts for a deposition? Does that change as to how you prepare them for cross-examinations?
Jeremy:	No, I would say not. At the expert's deposition, he or she should be ready to be cross-examined just as if it were a trial.

How you prepare, and this is an important point; it's necessary, whatever the topic, the lawyer, by the time you start preparing for the deposition, is as expert on the topic as the expert is. Otherwise, you're just not doing your job. When you're preparing for the deposition you have to know where the holes are. If you haven't thought about it, your expert might not think about it and he could get asked a question that will elicit an unhelpful response.

Ron: Do you work with your expert and strategize on how you're going to cross the adversary or depose the adversary?

Jeremy: You wouldn't show the expert the script. But you certainly want his or her view on where the holes are in the other expert's position.

Ron: Can an expert win or lose a case for you?

Jeremy: Absolutely. Your expert can be one of the most important witnesses to win the case, if not the most important to win. And if that expert doesn't have credibility on a particular matter and issue, the whole thing can fall apart.

Ron: Will you share a story where you've used an expert that was successful for you or your adversary's expert was not successful and why that was?

Jeremy: Your father is the perfect example.

Ron: Will you give us a little bit of background on that case?

Jeremy: It was a GAAP issue. How you account for a particular revenue or gain item in calculating an amount due under a particular lease provision. We know it's an area where there wasn't a clear answer in GAAP and we used that lack of clarity as the basis of our argument. If GAAP is not clear, then you need to look at what the underlying contract party has actually intended. Because if GAAP is clear, then the contract is not ambiguous when it references GAAP.

The other side was not effective at all because their entire argument depended on clarity in GAAP that just didn't exist. Ultimately, they had adopted a position that just wasn't tenable.

Ron: What advice do you give to the young associates about using financial experts?

Jeremy: The same advice I would give a young associate on anything, which is that what we do is more than a job and so treat it like that. You have to like to dig down into the case, including the matter on which you're having expert testimony, to such a thorough degree that you're prepared. You're as expert in it as the expert. Because if you don't do that, it will likely not turn out well.

Specifically, for young associates, I would say there's a tendency to be intimidated by the expert, intimidated by topics you don't know and you assume the expert knows it better than you; that's a bad assumption. Because, again, that can ultimately lead to the question not getting answered; questions that you need to know before you go in to have your expert testify.

www.ingramcontent.com/pod-product-compliance
Lightning Source LLC
Chambersburg PA
CBHW081240220326
41597CB00023BA/4220